Dear Sally,
    May you enjoy this
book as much as I enjoyed
writing it! God Bless You
Always!

Wander With Me ...

Poems by

Margaret Bergeron

"Wander each day of your Life
with Purpose, Faith and Love."
God Bless You!
    Margaret Bergeron

authorHOUSE®

AuthorHouse™
1663 Liberty Drive
Bloomington, IN 47403
www.authorhouse.com
Phone: 1-800-839-8640

First published by AuthorHouse 2/25/2010

ISBN: 978-1-4490-5646-9 (e)
ISBN: 978-1-4490-5645-2 (sc)
ISBN: 978-1-4490-5647-6 (hc)

Library of Congress Control Number: 2009913056

Printed in the United States of America
Bloomington, Indiana

WHAT YOU WILL FIND IN THIS BOOK

Faith

Love

Friends

Favorite Places

Feelings

Family

Parents

Children

Holidays

Grandchildren

Hope

Trust

Life

Comfort

Prayers

Introduction

From Her Beautiful Daughter...

Where do I start talking about the most amazing woman I know? She has inspired my every move. She has been there for me through every hard time and all the happy times. She was with me when my children (her grandchildren) were born and when I married the man of my dreams.

Her words have touched my very soul. I have witnessed the most amazing gift that GOD has given her. He writes through her. Her heart is bigger than the deepest ocean. Her words have touched thousands of lost souls. She has found the courage to write and then speak her words in front of total strangers and the closest of family. Though she might cry when she is speaking, she always gets through it.

My mom's words heal, they inspire, they touch, they comfort, they console, they reach deep into your heart and they grab a hold of your inner most thoughts and softly caress your soul.

It has been my dream for years to make this book for you. It has happened. Your words are here for the world to see. Everyone will finally get to see the gift we have had our whole lives. We are so lucky and blessed to have you.
All my love ALWAYS, **Cari**

From her Wonderful Son...

These expressions of a gentle love are representative of over a half a century of the ebbs and flows of a beautiful heart, that longs to touch the sometimes frozen, broken, anxious or overflowing thankful hearts of others....What a wondrous love is this! -**Donny**

From Her Loving, Amazing Husband...

She has been writing poems since we met years ago. She has been given the gift of words. I hold her in the highest esteem with the greats of the writing world, like, Lucado, John, Paul, Luke and many more.

You see, GOD inspires her words. She can sit under an oak tree, look at her surroundings, and see images that she turns into words. Once while driving, she saw clouds, trees and a forest, which became, **"Generations of Trees "**.

She sees beyond the chairs rocking on the porch, she sees the people who sat in the chairs so long ago. She does not see the old hands holding purses, she sees the hands holding the granddaughter's face and kissing her cheek, or holding the freshly washed baby in the soft blanket. She sees the face of the Veteran, sun baked, scarred by time, and troubled by life, and she sees his heart. Margaret has a favorite verse in the bible. "Be still and know that I am GOD". She understands that completely. When GOD speaks, she listens.

She is the love of my life. **-Billy**

Dedication

I dedicate this book, first...to God, who is The One who gave me the words and the inspiration to write. To my wonderful, giving parents, John and Clarice, who taught me to write, together with my brothers, Johnny, Tom, and Michael, for pushing me to do something with my poems. To my spectacular husband, Billy, who continues to give me the love, support and the encouragement to write. To our beautiful Children, Cari and Donny, with their wonderful spouses, Les and Melissa, who have given me the "need" and the "want" to write. To our wonderful Grandchildren, Billy, Nicholas, Kerra, Matthew, and Kaela, Aaron, Alicia, and Great-Grandchildren, Autumn and Davy, who keep me filled with awe and provide me with moments to reflect upon. To my gracious family and friends who have listened intently at every holiday and event that they have ever attended, and allowed me to read my poems aloud. To the Editors of the Mobile Home News, Rick and Linda, that gave me the chance to write poems in their newspaper, in my column "WANDER WITH ME", and to all the faithful readers that enjoyed the words and helped them to reflect on their lives. This book is a reflection of how I feel "inside". Thank you ALL for letting me bring it "outside". This is truly one of the DREAMS of my life. The first DREAM is my husband, Billy... He was the man of my dreams in high school and continues to be my hero for more than 42 years. Thank you for listening to me and believing in me for so many years...**I love you...**

Margaret

IN LOVING MEMORY of JOHNNY McCLINTON

JOHNNY...

Johnny, Johnny, what can I say...?To a special brother like you...?
You have a warm spot in my heart...Your love was oh, so true...
You always were so kind to all...Your words and eyes said so much...
Everyone, even cats and dogs...Responded to your soft touch...

You were a lover of many things...Beauty and plants and life...
God had truly filled your soul...In spite of all your strife...
You've come a long way in years...Than most could ever do...
You really were the strong one...Yes, Johnny, I mean you...

I'd never written you a poem...But, my poems were a lot about you...
People like you, encouraged me...In what I tried to do...
You always gave me the strokes...That all of us need to hold...
That special "push" to help me through...In times I could turn cold...

We had a lot of problems...Of every imaginable kind...
Money and moving and aching and cars...
But, God helped us, so we didn't mind...
You kept your neat disposition...Your humor,
your laughter, your smile...
And all those years were surely blessed...
Because we stayed close all the while...
Johnny, now you are with Our Lord...You're hearing us all today...
We always will remember you...And everything you had to say...
So with a smile, I'll dry my tears...And think of you up above...
Because...Heaven embraces our brother...
And he holds our special love...

I always loved to hear your voice...On the other end of the phone...
No matter what our struggles were...No matter what the tone...
We couldn't spend much time together...But when we got to meet...
It was like no gap between us lay...And our visit was "Oh, so sweet"...

Written for Johnny, By your Sister, Margaret

July 16, 1994

The night after your funeral, Mom had a dream about you walking up to her in a brand new white suit. She said you were smiling and that you said you were not sick anymore, and not to worry. God gave her that dream so that they could continue to go on...Thank God for that, will you?

1998... It's been four years since I wrote this poem....My thoughts have not changed much...
I still miss you every day...And I see the lives you've touched...
Looking at your pictures and such....WE ALL STILL MISS YOU VERY MUCH...

2001...I FINALLY FINSHED...although there is so much more to your life than just seven pages, the rest will just stay in our hearts.. .until we meet again...

2009...I am finally publishing my book, dedicated in memory of you....
Love, Margaret

From his niece, Cari ...
To my sweet Uncle Johnny. You are always in our hearts. Your gift was to teach us to be kind and loving souls. You are greatly missed and loved by all who knew you, but especially by my mom, your little sister. You are still inspiring and your spirit is always close by to give us comfort. I will always remember the "Cricket" and your "Conga Drums". Your smile I will always hold close to my heart. - **Cari**

START WITH JUST A LITTLE DREAM…

Start with just a little dream…
Water it each day…
Give it love and nourishment…
Don't let it slip away…

Watch it grow and multiply…
Don't let it out the door…
If others try to stop you…
Just strive to want it more…

A dream needs your protection…
'Cause it will bloom some day…
Hold it closely to your heart…
It will be safe that way…

The day will come, and you will see…
What happens with patience and care…
That "little dream" you dreamed that day…
Will blossom everywhere…

So, don't give up, no matter what…
Be persistent in every way…
'Cause with God's help and lots of love…
That "little dream" will be "real" some day…

Written by Margaret Bergeron
About my "Little Dream"…
August 1997

FORGET YOU...NEVER...

Some people touch your lives...
The way no others could...
Securing a place within your heart...
Where it's warm and safe and good...

Some people know your feelings...
Know what to say and do...
To make your day more cheery...
And easier for you...

You know the ones I talk about...
You sigh as you hear their voice...
The smile and grin you love to see...
The ones you'd pick, by choice...

You pray they'll always be there...
To come and stand by you...
To try to lend a helping hand...
No matter what you do...

The same ones you rely on...
Depend upon YOUR care...
Whenever they are needing...
To also have you there...

Can't imagine life without them...
No matter what they do...
Knowing people just like them...
Make you lucky being you...

People come and people go...
Some feelings go forever...
No matter here or heaven...
Could you forget them...Never...

Written by Margaret Bergeron
2001

MY FOREVER LOVE...

We have come...oh so far...
I can't begin to think...
42 whole years of love...
Have gone by in a wink...
Today, as I think of all...
Our family and friends...
God has blessed us with both...
Plus, HIS love is without end...
We've had trials in 42 years...
And, gotten through them all...
Because we have a Savior...
Picking us up, when we would fall...
"Me Mi Lo"...three special words...
We made up secretly...
Simple little words that mean...
Please, "Never Leave Me"...
To say you've made me happy...
To say there's been some sad...
There's been a mix of everything...
The best blessing I've ever had...
You are the only present...
That I will ever crave...
Loving, smart & give great hugs...
And, you're very, very brave...
42 years ago, today...
So young and scared and new...
I'm so happy and proud right now...
Just standing next to you...
Happy Anniversary Billy...
And just to tell a "speck"
I still get goose bumps every time...
You kiss me on my neck!!!...
You are the Love of my life...My blessing from God...Our
Children's hero...Thank you for so many wonderful years...

Margaret xoxox
April 8, 2009

SMILE AT YOUR FUTURE

We don't know what the future holds…
Don't know how long we'll stay…
Don't know about tomorrow…
Would we change it anyway…?

Don't know just what is happening…
Our world is so unsure…
Try to keep the peace and then…
We worry about a war…

So, since we don't exactly know…
What tomorrow's day will bring…
Smile and love the present…
We're children of God, Our King…

We maybe don't know the future…
But at least we know it's true…
Exactly "Who" holds it for us…
In heaven, for me and you…

Written by Margaret Bergeron
March 2003

IF YOU FORGET TO PRAY…

When you think, your heart will break…
When you feel you cannot sleep…
It's time to give your ALL to God…
In HIS Heart it's okay to weep…

He'll hold you in His Great Big Arms…
He'll rock you asleep so fast…
If you will just believe and trust…
Your fears will become your past…

When you <u>cannot</u> get it all done…
Or a deadline you can't meet…
What more or what else can you do…?
Just bring it to OUR LORD'S feet…

He told us to depend on HIM…
Thru HIM…to do all things…
But still we try to do it alone…
And all the turmoil it brings…

You wake up with good intentions…
"You'll get it all done today"…
By night, you're pooped and out of time…
All because…YOU FORGOT TO PRAY…

Written by Margaret Bergeron
December 2003

DOWN THAT TRAIL...

If you've been traveling on a path...
Not going very far...
Satisfied to stay real close...
"Pretty happy" with where you are...

Not putting too much effort...
With staying a "step ahead"...
Not really on the "plus" side...
But "not quite" in the red...

Stepping a little "to or fro"...
Could tip the apple cart...
You're staying "exactly" where you're "set"...
Keeping dreams "only" in your heart...

Take a little step outside...
"Beyond" your comfort zone...
You may see some dreams come true...
More "successes" of your own...

When you think "you can't do more"...
It's easier to lie...
Worried that you just might "fail"...
And so...you just don't try...

We're given many blessings...
We could "never" use them all...
Take a "risk" while on that trail...
"Get up", if you should fall...

Some dreams come true...some do not...
And you'll never wonder why...
If you say a prayer and take a step...
At least give it a try...

Written by Margaret Bergeron

NO MORE CONFUSION…!

He tells her one thing...Then he does another...
He acted concerned...Now he can't bother...

Making her crazy...She's not sure where to turn...
No wonder that she thinks...That he'll never learn...

Breaking his vows...Ruining his son...
Not caring who...Is hurt on the run...

Living a sham...All of his life...
Being deceptive...To his loving wife...

Lying and cheating...Playing the con...
Changing his mind...Putting her on...

On with her life...A brand new start...
Take a deep breath….Then take hold of your heart...

You did all you could...When the truth had been found...
God knew your intention...Was to turn things around...

But he broke the covenant...Between God, man and wife...
He'll be the one responsible...For all of his life...

Don't mess with God's -Law...It's written in stone...
And… there for a purpose...No way to postpone...!

Written by Margaret Bergeron
May 1998

BEHIND THOSE LOVING EYES...

There is a man that worries so...
Behind those loving eyes...
The kind that say, "don't leave, don't go"...
His heart and mind, so wise...

The same man thinks of problems...
And how they will survive...
Where did all his hard work go...?
When he worked nine to five...

Those soft blue eyes look deep at you...
As you say, "What's new today?"...
As if they were trying to figure out...
What you're going to do or say...

A glance at him recently, showed me a side...
I didn't quite know what to think...
It scared me a bit, because I love him so...
Then he chased fears away with one wink...

No matter what age your parent may be...
Or even if they aren't around...
Remember the look behind those loving eyes...
All the love you have missed will be found...

Written by Margaret Bergeron
December 1997

A LITTLE OLDER...

It was my Birthday...
And how do I feel?
A little bit older...
But, that's no big deal...
I have much more...
Than most, I'll agree...
A husband I love...
And a great family...

A home that we live in...
A nice car that I drive...
Clothes on my back...
Happy to, be alive...
A wonderful daughter, terrific son...
With spouses that love them, too...
Six grandchildren, we have in all...
No reason to ever be blue...

Sometimes we need a moment...
To remember what we've got...
So. right now, I'll say "THANK YOU"...
You've all given me a lot...
Who could ask for more than this..?
Expressing myself as I write...
Viewing the world as a background...
Letting go of them, like a kite...

So, having a birthday's not so bad...
As long as you all come along...
WANDER WITH ME... through the journey...
Sharing feelings, like singing a song...
So, yes, I'm a little older...
But a whole lot richer, too...
Every day that I wake up...
I thank God for all of you...

Love, Margaret Bergeron
Written March 20, 1999

EVER WONDER WHY?

Did you ever wonder why...God gave you a little boy...?
Ever wonder what He planned...When creating this tiny joy...?

Was it only for your pride...To carry on your name...?
To share the sports and manly things...So,
Dad and Son could be the same...?

Was it planned for teaching...Your son, to be prepared...?
For all the things life brings him...To pray when he is scared...?

To show him how to love his Mom...To give example to his Sis..?
How to teach his family some day...Guide those who go amiss...?

Give the principles of life to him...?Teach him how to pray...?
To lavish him with spiritual gifts...?Even as you play...?

To let him know right from the start...His goal in life is grand..?
To show responsibility...While taking a firm stand...?

Should you also show him...How much you love his Mom...?
How to cherish and forgive...?Just like you do, my son...?

So, look upon your little son...So precious and so new...
He's pleasing to your family...No wonder, God gave him to you...!

Written by "Mom" Margaret Bergeron
March 1999

JUST FOR BEING THERE...

Doctors, Stuff and Nurses...At our UCLA...
Truly are amazing...What you can do today...
Not only are you geniuses...In how you use your mind...
You take the time in every way...To treat your patient's kind...
It seems you have an insight...On how the families feel...

You surely go the extra mile...Helping ALL of us to heal...
Even in the foodplace...Cafeteria or Cafe'...
Tiverton House Hotel was great...What a wonderful place to stay...
"Dedication" is the word...Focusing on the cure...

Finding yet a better way...Practicing... making sure...
Do we even know how hard...Medical Professionals work...?
Doctors,. Nurses, Assistants...Custodial, Reception and Clerk...
It takes a lot of know-how...Immense compassion, too...

Helping people every day...There's no end to all you do...
We saw a real "TEAM" working...When you cared for our 'Dear Dad"...
Your gentle kindness, made us feel...He was the "only" patient you had...
School can teach procedures...Calculations too...

But you combine it with caring...Teaching students while you do...
Looking to each person's eyes...Give a hug, or hold a hand....
Who knows, you may be giving...Something someone never had...
No one ever forgot to smile...Or give a "comfort touch"...

We never felt out of control...Your confidence meant so much...
You remembered our family...Leaning against the wall...
Our loved one was in surgery...We paced up and down the hall...
The smiles of your acknowledgment...Is all we looked to find...

Giving hope to saddened eyes...It eased our troubled mind...
We know you see a lot of folks...Which is why I am writing too...
You ALL came forward to help us cope...
Thank you ALL for all that you do...!!
With so much thanks to all of you at UCLA...For taking such good care of

John H McClinton, Our Dad, Husband, Grandpa and Great-Grandpa
With love and thanks from our whole family.

Written By Margaret Bergeron (Daughter)
August 1999

GIVE SOME EXTRA BLESSINGS

Give some extra blessings Lord..
To hearts that hurt today...
Give some extra courage and strength...
To those that have gone astray...

Give to those less fortunate...
A place to lay their head...
When it's cold or rainy out...
Provide for them a bed...

Give to those in pain each day...
Some hours of reprieve...
Help your children in distress...
Let them hold on to your sleeve...

Open up the hearts of those...
Who do not know your grace...
Slow them down and give them hope...
And a new life to embrace...

Remind us that your love for us...
Is more than the grains of the sand...
We are safe inside your heart...
We are held in the Palm of Your Hand...

And when we think we know it all...
Or can do it on our own...
Give us Some Extra Blessings Lord...
And "One more stepping stone"...

Written by Margaret Bergeron
March 1998

GOD'S LETTER

God's written many letters…As the Bible verses say…
If He were to write another one…This is "PROBABLY WHAT HE'D SAY"
"TO MY DEAREST CHILDREN"
"You need to cling together…Help each other all you can…"

"Never let the moment pass…Help children, woman and man…"
"Things that sometimes happen…Make your love and friendships grow…"
"Peace could grow across our country…You just never, ever know…"
"If only you could see the world…From where I look at you…"

You'd wonder why you didn't try…To change the things you do…"
"My children, you were put here…To serve each other's needs…"
"Not just when a disaster comes, are you to do good deeds…"
HE'D PROBABLY SAY:
"Every day, you have a chance…To show what's in your heart…"

"Let go of your possessions…Stop tearing each other apart…"
"You cannot take them with you…I know that for a fact…"
"Cause if you could, there would be no room…Heaven would be packed…"
HE'D PROBABLY SAY:
"I see some people stealing…And hoarding all they can…"

"Right next to someone starving…Instead of
Sharing with their fellow man…"
"I created this whole universe…There's so much room for all…"
"I gave you the right to make choices…My
Heart breaks when I see you fall…"
"When I see you love each other…Letting others in your heart…"

"Then, My Sunsets mean the most…You include ME from the start…"
AND GOD WOULD PROBABLY SAY:
"I'm so proud of all the good…That I see you do each day…"

"I'm preparing a special place for you…In Heaven, if that's okay…?"
"You are MY children, all of you…I made
You with MY OWN HANDS…"
'NO ONE LOVES YOU MORE THAN ME…"
"SOMEDAY, YOU'LL UNDERSTAND…!"
AND GOD WOULD SURELY SAY:

"I LOVE YOU FOREVER… GOD"

Written by Margaret Bergeron…September 2005

TRY

We should try to love all people...
There's some good in everyone...
By trying this, we soon will find...
Our troubles on the run...

Look for the love in people...
It's sometimes hard to do...
But life will treat you better...
If you TRULY use this view...

Not one of us is without faults...
Surely, we should bear in mind...
That we are not so different...
And, we want to be treated kind...

Beware of cutting others down...
This is oh, so wrong...
"Love your neighbor as yourself"...
(You <u>knew</u> that all along)...

The many different cultures here...
Shouldn't cause us to drift apart...
Because, all of us are really the same...
Just look inside your heart...

Written by Margaret Bergeron

LET"S NOT FORGET

During this special holiday...
With all the gifts and fun...
That the "Reason for the Season"...
Is the birth of Our Lord's Son...

All the food and preparation...
The table set just right...
Give thanks for all your blessings...
Each day and every night...

Look at gifts beneath the tree...
Be grateful they are there...
You were able to buy them...
Which shows how much you care...

Gaze into your loved ones eyes...
Before they're tucked in bed...
Share the meaning of this day...
With some of the words you read...

By your example every day...
You can change the meaning more...
Than spending "hundreds" worth on things...
At some department store...

So for this day. I'm praying for...
God's blessings from above...
For all my family and friends...
My gift is... "All My Love"...

Written by Margaret Bergeron
December 1997

WAITING, WONDERING AND WISHING..

Waiting and wondering and wishing...
What's just around the bend...?
Looking at your calendar...
Wishing summer wouldn't end...

What to cook for dinner...
Wishing to make it late…
Wonder who is on the phone...
Waiting for that special date...

Wondering what the next day brings...
Waiting for a ride...
Wondering where the time flies...
Waiting for the tide...

Wonder how the children grow...
Waiting for a "sign"...
Wishing you could just relax...
Waiting to be 'just fine"...

Waiting for the doctor..,
Wishing you hadn't come...
Wondering why you have to age...
Wishing you had some gum...

Wishing well to loved ones...
Wondering how you cope...
Waiting for a call return...
And a tiny ray of hope...

Waiting, wondering and wishing...
Is what you <u>DO</u> each day...
None of it makes any sense...
If you don't take time to pray...

Written by Margaret Bergeron
January 1998

DAYS THAT WE'LL REMEMBER MOST...

The days that we'll remember most...
Are the ones we spend with you...
Driving up to anywhere...
Just out to dinner will do...

Laughing, talking, about life...
How things used to be...
Wondering how we've come this far...
How God has helped you, and "we"...

How a family matters most...
When you need an ear to hear...
How a phone call, from far away...
Can surely bring a tear...

Thinking how we love to be...
Around you all the time...
Wondering why my brain is always...
Thinking of a rhyme...

How we are so blessed to have...
A family like we do...
Being with our Mom and Dad...
Could truly bless you, too...

God has held our hands together...
And given us love to share...
Thank you for being so special...
And for always being there...

Written by Margaret Bergeron
July 2001

FOG IN HIS LIFE...

He didn't want to hurt you...
He's such a troubled soul...
Fighting with his limited strength...
Has surely taken its toll...

This child of God is so confused...
He's surely lost his way...
Through the Fog in his young life...
It has filled his weary days...

Thought he could control it...
Thought he had the upper hand...
Forgot his "Opposition"...
Is alive throughout the land...

When you have a Fog within your life...
Covering all you do...
Without some help, you can't climb out...
It covers your family, too...

We send our prayers and wishes...
Letters and so much love...
But, the only thing that REALLY helps...
Prayer and strength from God above...

Written By Margaret Bergeron
August 2001

18

KEEP LOVE ON TOP...

If you keep your mind too open...Your brains will sure fall out...
If you forget God in your life...You'll be left, there is no doubt...
If anger grows within your heart...Comes out from your own voice...
Saying words that hurt or burn...Not speaking...is your choice...

Be in each others service...Should be a main concern...
Let God's peace rule in your hearts...And for His graces, yearn...
Looking for someone to blame...For troubles that occur...
Does not claim a victory...No contentment, that's for sure...

The secret to claiming victory...Over prejudice and pride...
Is more Humility and Love...With Jesus as your guide...
The one who has the most great toys...Still sees a Judgment Day...
Those riches, cars and gadgets...Won't pave a clearer way...

God wants you to be happy...A good job, house and clothes...
Just let your first priority...Be God's Kingdom, BEFORE those...
God takes care of tomorrows, too...Live only for today...
Don't worry and don't wonder...It won't help in any way...

Be content with what you have...Don't get caught up in pride...
Don't be selfish, vain or smug...Stay on the humble side...
We've struggled with these feelings...Every single day...
Because we are just human...And, God made us this way...

If you can put Love on the top...Of EVERYTHING you do...
Then, anger, blame and prejudice...Will have NO claim on you...!

Written by Margaret Bergeron
May 2001

A STONE TO THROW...

Many songs sing feelings...To being "down and out"...
Many poems say the words...Here's what its all about...

Many, many years ago...A Man said "throw a stone"...
"All you without a blemish"..."To one that stands alone"...

If there is even one out there...That never made a blunder...
Then let the heavens clap for them...And add a little thunder...

Make a big mistake some day...And hope you'll not be scorned...
EVERYBODY makes them...So better be forewarned...

Some are on the "good" side...As long as "good" they do...
Better not be "bragging"...Someday you will goof, too!!!

All the "good" that you may do...Goes "Unnoticed" to some degree...
But dare "Disturb the apple cart"...And a "victim" you will be...

Beat a man or hurt his pride...Takes his spirit, drive and will...
Talk behind his humble back...Can hurt him further still...

A moral to this story ... Remember, when you hurt, too...
"Atta boy" or "Job well done'...Makes a better man Out of you...

AND...

If you think you are without a fault...Or pick up a stone to throw...
It will return to you someday...Just ask someone who knows...

Written by Margaret Bergeron
July 1998

A DAY IN THE LIFE...

Sometimes they start at 4:00 am...How ever do they wake...?
Working hard, right through the day...Such abuse, they have to take...
Reading plans, digging holes...Pulling wire, laying pipe...
Cement pours and hauling rock...Skip loader/backhoe type...
Everyone is moving...The minute that they enter...
One day it is just plain, flat dirt...The next, a Storage Center...!
Permits from the city...Then, inspectors come...
Checking all electric...Saying, "it is OR "is not" done...
Dirt is flying everywhere...Trucks taking soil away...

Stakes are set, markers up...Just another part of their day...
Keeping owners happy...Meeting deadlines too...
Doesn't seem like much to us...But to them, it's what they do...
Making sense of blueprints...Changing walls or grades...
Hammers, nails and skill saws...With hundreds of new blades...
Someone's GOT to plan it out...Someone's GOT to run the job...
Someone's GOT to check for kinks...So
SOMEONE ELSE can turn the knob...
It takes a lot of "Know How"...To get it all together...

It takes a lot of patience...When you don't have good weather...
Some choose to be the Leaders...Others want to wear a cap...
What it really takes is "TEAM WORK"...
To build a "Blue Printed Map"...
Sometimes life gets hectic...Going many different ways...
Schedules, plans and architects...Things changing every day...
That is why it means so much...That you take the time to care...
Planned a special time for your Company...And for families to be there...
We could tell, how hard you worked at it...
From the food, to the funny games...

Making everyone comfortable...And (almost) remembering our names...!
The girls in the office worked so hard...The cooks, they worked hard too...
Even though the "sausage" burned me...(I promise not to sue...!)
Thank you for the prizes...Bingo, the races and all...
Especially, the visual memory...Of the "Tu Tu's" and Golf Balls...
It is very evident TO ALL...Your Company is a "TEAM"...
Working and playing together...Is exactly as it seems...
So, before I get too corny...we'll simply, once more, say...

Thank you for remembering us...and...Thanks for the wonderful day...!
Bill and Margaret Bergeron...*By Margaret Bergeron August 2001*

FAMILY

Whatever happens in our life...
However far we roam...
We never go too far from where...
We feel we have a home...
Troubles, joys and stresses...
Happen to all of us...
Tears and fears just go away...
When a loved one wants to fuss...

Open arms with hugs and kisses...
Time gone just melts away...
No matter how long it has been...
They beg for you to stay...
There's no limit to the joy...
That your children bring to you...
Each of their lives are so attached..
To all the things you do...

Imagining a life without..
The joys of family ties....
Just wouldn't be complete at all...
It brings tears to my eyes...
So if you have a family...
Whether here or far away...
Never let a day go by...
Without giving some love away...

We never know about tomorrow...
And we let go of the past...
We should live today, as if...
It were to be our last...

Written by Margaret Bergeron
July 1997

WHAT WILL THEY SAY?...

When you are not here...
What will they say...?
What thoughts will they think...
When you pass away...?
It's not so bad to talk about...
What you do throughout your days...
After all, it is YOUR LIFE...
That tells them what to say...

Have you been a good example...
To all that you hold dear...?
Have you been a guiding light...
Have your morals been real clear...?
Do you tell your family...
With words as well as show.,,?
Everything they mean to you...
Every day...wherever you go...?

Do you hold a grudge on one...?
Or shun another too...?
It would feel so great to let it go...
It would be so good for you...
When you look back, on your life...
And what you'd think they'd say...
Hoping for good and positive...
And not another way...

You know, it's not too late for you...
You still have many days...
Make amends with all you know...
Then, you'll KNOW "What They Will Say"...

Written by Margaret Bergeron
February 23, 2000

DON'T WASTE A SINGLE MINUTE..

Don't waste a single minute...
Of life's most precious day...
Don't ever wait too long to do...
Nice things...sweet words to say..
Look upon the sunny side...
Don't let an hour be bleak...
Take every opportunity...
Everyday of every week...
Practice changing your attitude...
Work at your self esteem...
Get in sync with workers...
With your family... be a team...
Take one big step in every day...
To make your lifetime sing...
Do whatever you need to do...
There's nothing you need to bring...
Every time you wake up...
Start with a smile and prayer...
Chase your worries out of town...
Be with the ones that care...
Surround yourself with laughter...
But, leave some room to cry...
Things can happen in our lives...
Babies are born, and loved ones die...
If you have a loved one...
Don't waste a single minute...
Forget about tomorrow....
Today is the day...you're in it!...
A hug, a call, a loving word...
Help everyone you can...
Never let a day go by...
Without lending a gentle hand...

Written by Margaret Bergeron
January 1999

GETTING THROUGH THE DAY...

All I ask of you Dear Lord...is...
Get me through this day...
Take away anxiety...
Show me some other way...

Substitute a peace of mind...
Alleviate the stress...
Help me sort out problems...
That got me in this mess...

Let my eyes see clearer...
So I can take a step...
Put a halt to sadness...
So I will have some pep...

Knowing You will help me...
Is all I need to know...
Getting through this day's been tough...
Just thought I'd tell you so...

Nothing I can't handle...
As long as I have You...
Ups and downs evaporate...
You know just what to do...

Written By Margaret Bergeron
July 2000

A GOOD SAMARITAN...

Remembering each day is new...Never knowing what will be...
Needing a "Good Samaritan"...Could sure be you or me...

God made every one of us...All different, but the same...
Every person special...With a different name...

Don't know when you may need one...You pray you never will...
You could be down and out on luck...Some choices haunt you still...

If you were on the "other" side...Seeking kindness from a friend....
That someone could just pass you by...Their hand they would not lend...

What if you had no food to eat...No place to rest your head...
Couldn't bathe or have clean clothes...Or sleep in your cozy bed...

What if people closed their eyes...Like they didn't even care...?
What if they whispered in disgust...?Not caring you were there...?

How would you feel about just "one"...Who took the "time" to stop...?
Cared for all your pain and loss...From the bottom to the top...

If you could help a battered soul,...Give a soothing, helping hand...
Keep hurting words from spreading...Show empathy while you can..

There's ALWAYS something you can do...Just open up your heart...
Be a "GOOD SAMARITAN"...That's the greatest place to Start...

Written by Margaret Bergeron.
September 2000

WORN OUT SHOES...

If you look past a poor man's shoes...
And deep within his heart...
You will find a person there...
That is where our help should start...

If he was your brother...
Would you leave him with no food..?
Walk right by, with not a glance...?
Pretend he was no good....?

It's easier to turn away...
Step over, try not to see...
Keep the warm and fuzzy things...
It's easy to agree...

It could be any one of us...
Out there, in despair...
Would you want to be stepped over...
Or hope someone would care...?

Sure, they may be faking...
Making more money than you...
Some will try to trick and scheme...
How about the ones that are true...?

So, if you give to ten in all...
And only one was true...
Forget about the nine who lied...
That "one" sure needed you...

Written by Margaret Bergeron
October 1999

WHAT'S WAITING...?

We really don't know what is waiting...
Only around the next bend...
You cannot prepare for the happenings...
Before they're about to begin...

One person is sick or is ailing...
Another is well and just fine...
One minute we're great, the next we are not.....
The Lord does not give us a sign...

No matter what shape your "condition" is in...
How healthy or sick or unfit...
Just live out today, like it was your last...
With love and prayers, vigor and wit...

Your years could be.. 10 or past 90...
Doesn't matter what number your age...
Bring out the happiness, way deep inside...
Push out feelings of anger or rage...

There's really no room, in our hearts for bad things...
It only brings turmoil and strife...
When bad things are gone, the good can return...
To give us a quality life...

We have no control over "quantity"...
That's something that's figured "before"...
We were given "10" rules we should live by...
To guide us through...forevermore...

Written by Margaret Bergeron
November 1998

WHEN THE CHIPS ARE DOWN...

When the chips are down...get right back up...
Put your whole life on that track...
Don't look behind ...just straight ahead...
Never, ever wander back...

There's bumps to come ...and on the way...
There's many roads to go...
Say your prayers and forge ahead....
Otherwise, you'll never know...

Cause when your "chips" are falling...
You really are at the start...
Of picking up and brushing the dust...
That surrounds your tender heart..

No matter what your problem....
Whether it is big or small...
You'll find you can get through it...
Some day, through it all...

It doesn't feel too good right now...
But soon it will feel right...
Let the sun shine in and smile...
Give a chance to make it bright...

Make yourself a good friend first...
And you will one day find...
That you will help somebody...
While giving you peace of mind...

Written by Margaret Bergeron
April 1999

A BRAND NEW START

His compassions never fail...
Every morning they are new...
No matter what your past has held...
It's a Brand New Start for you...
No matter what torments your heart...
No matter where you've roamed...
Even if you think you're lost...
You're very close to Home...
The past is what it sounds like...
Yesterday is gone...
God is reaching out His Hand...
Saying "please, won't you hold on"...?
The farther that you roam from God...
Makes you need Him even more...
Turning your back, walking away...
Has hurt down to the core...
The longer that you stay away...

You think you can't go back...
But He is <u>still</u> there waiting....
No matter what you lack...
How can God forgive us...?
For we <u>do</u> surely sin..
Turn our hearts and mind from Him...
And He <u>still</u> lets us in...!
We can be in the very pit...
When you see no pathway out...
Darkness lurking all around...
Like God tells us about...
You think you have no right to step...
Up the ladder to the top...
Hanging your head with sadness...
Then FORGIVENESS pulls you up...
Our God's compassions never fail...

Every morning they are new..
No matter what your path has held...
It's a "Brand New Start" for you...

Written by Margaret Bergeron...2003

YOUR PURPOSE...

If you take God from your daily life...
The days would make no sense...
The nights and weeks so empty...
Your pain much more intense...
If you could live your every day...
Knowing "why" you have come to be...
That you were "made" for God to love...
For all eternity...

If you're trying to find your purpose...
Then, you "must" get to know...
The God who first created you...
He'll show you where to go...
It's never, ever too late to be...
Who you "might" have been...
Start with finding your purpose...
Beginning with God...just Him...

Begin by reading the manual...
That shows you how you're made...
The "only" Book that shows you how...
God's great plans were laid...
Inside you'll find your purpose...
The blueprint of your life ...
No other book could match the words...
That the Bible will put in your life...

The first step is always the hardest...
Be courageous when you walk...
Don't let another hold you back...
Don't be afraid to talk...
And when your body is all used up...
And your time on earth is done...
God's made a home for you...
Where we all can live as one...

Written by Margaret Bergeron
October 13, 2002

A HEALING PRAYER...

Dear God...
Sometimes pain can be severe...
Overwhelming the body and mind...
Sometimes I lose my sight of YOU...
Leaving YOU way behind...

When illness, pain and troubles...
Come to jumble up the day...
Clouding up my daily life...
YOU help me get away...

Away to just a quiet place...
Only YOU and I can go...
To pray for healing comfort...
Because YOU love me so...

YOU free me from my burdens...
To make my faith so strong...
YOU told me I could trust in YOU...
And YOU cannot be wrong...

LORD, help to heal this body...
Or give me strength to bear...
Whatever YOU would have for me...
I know YOU'RE always there...

Most of all remind me...
To put my all in YOU...
To be cheerful while I pray today...
Like YOU would want me to...

Written by Margaret Bergeron
April 2002

ALL ALONE...WITH YOU...

As I sit here all alone…
Alone with YOU, My Lord…
I wonder what YOU'D have me say…?
Give me the perfect word…

May YOUR life be glorified…
May our prayers be heard…
Above the busy chaos…
May we cling to every word…

So many hearts are aching…
So many souls seem lost…
GOD, please open up their lives…
No matter what the cost…

Give extra strength to those who mourn…
To those, that are so ill…
Help to heal the broken hearts…
Dear GOD, I know you will…

Our parents and our children…
Our siblings and our pets…
Our troops who fight and lose their lives…
Can the war be finished yet…?

Dear Lord, give us YOUR vision…
As clear as clear can be…
To let us know just what to do…
So that we can clearly see…

And if it's not too much to ask…
Can YOU grant our prayers this day…?
For tomorrow we will have some more…
And a whole new day to pray…

AMEN

Written and composed by Margaret Bergeron
June 2005

THANK YOU...

I CANNOT BEGIN TO TELL YOU...
HOW MUCH IT MEANS TO ME...
HOW WRITING WORDS OF LOVE AND FAITH...
COULD FILL AN EMPTY SEA...

HOW HEARING THAT YOU CARE SO MUCH...
ENCOURAGES ME THE MORE...
PUSHES OUT THE WORDS AND RHYMES...
AND TOUCHES ME TO THE CORE...

SO MANY THINGS HAVE HAPPENED...
IN "ALL OUR COUNTRIES" LIVES...
MAKE US VALUE FREEDOM...
CHILDREN, HUSBANDS AND WIVES...

MAKE US VALUE FRIENDSHIPS...
THE JOBS AND FOOD WE EAT...
SEEING PEOPLE WE CARE ABOUT...
WHEN WALKING DOWN THE STREET...

READING OUR HOME PAPER...
BRINGS TEARS INTO OUR EYES...
TO ALL THE THINGS AROUND US...
WE "ALL" HAVE EMOTIONAL TIES...

I WANT, AGAIN, TO SAY TO YOU...
YOUR WORDS HAVE MADE MY DAY...
THANK YOU FOR LETTING ME WRITE TO YOU...
IN THIS VERY SPECIAL WAY...

GOD BLESS YOU ALL...
MARGARET BERGERON
September 21, 2001

GOD CAME IN...

I sat there, praying in that room...
Afraid of what would be...
The doorway opened by itself...
God came to be with me...

The test was hard to go through...
The pain was so severe...
God held my husband's hand so tight...
Who held my hand so dear...

And while the tears were flowing...
Though it was nearly done...
I knew that we got comfort...
From, the Greatest One...

And though we didn't see His Face...
We surely felt His care...
And also felt His Hands in ours...
Yes, He was really there...

And as I write this poem today...
Remembering with a grin...
I always will remember...
The day that God came in...

Written by Margaret Bergeron
June 2003

OUR HOLIDAY PRAYER...

Lord, help us to remember...
To thank You every day...
For all that you have given us...
And, sometimes, take away...

You guide us from temptations...
Sort out our problems too...
You give "free will" to mess things up...
If that's what we "choose" to do...

You gave to us this great big world...
With oceans, flowers and trees...
You made us to love and cherish and care...
Feel the warmth, the cold and the breeze...

You didn't forget the mountains and lakes...
The deserts, the valleys, the sky...
We do not deserve Your Wondrous Love...
We get Blessings without asking why...

We thank You for parents, our family, our kids...
For neighbors and friends that we know...
For husbands and wives and our favorite pets...
And for letting the love in us grow...

We thank You for people that help us each day...
For rainbows, the rain and the snow...
Especially for shining the sun everywhere...
And a place for Your moon to go...

You've given so many blessings...
Surely, we've left out a few...
"Thank You" for the food that's awaiting us now...
Bless the hands that "prepared" it too...

Written by Margaret Bergeron...1998

INDEPENDENCE CAKE...

Take a gallon of freedom...
Add a pound of space...
Melt a little powder blue...
Put the sky up in its place...

Sprinkle in some color...
Flowers, mountains, trees...
Take a pinch of river and lakes...
Blend to make a breeze...

Knead it with ability...
Let it rise till you have hope...
Add the gift of friendship...
And patience to help you cope...

Gather everyone around...
Every race and creed...
Holding hands and giving thanks...
For our "Independence" need...

Try this yummy recipe...
And I just have a hunch...
You'll start out with an empty bowl...
And end up with a bunch...

Think of all that you can do...
All the things that you can add...
Add some clouds and sunshine...
That would not be bad...

Each recipe can differ...
In this "Independence Cake"...
"LOVE" is the main ingredient...
Without, it just won't bake...

Written by Margaret Bergeron
July 1999

MINI HOLIDAY...

Sitting by the poolside...
Soaking up the sun...
Visiting our long time friends...
For a week of fun...

Took a while to get here...
Drove through hours of rain...
Stopped to get a bite to eat...
Then on the road again...

Trying to unwind a bit...
From life's most hectic ways...
Takes a while to just relax...
When you leave behind those days...

Just a "little bit" on our own...
Before we must return...
Gonna put some sunscreen on...
So that our skin won't burn...

We took this mini-holiday...
(Suggest you take one too)...
Getting away from daily "things"...
Will "shoo" the blues from you...

Written by Margaret Bergeron
September 1998

ST. PAT'S DAY...

We had a 'bit of a party...
Saint Patrick's Day, the theme...
We feasted on corned beef and cabbage...
Potatoes, salad and ice cream...

A 'top of the mornin' to ya...
That's what the Irish say...
"Oh Danny Boy" was among the tunes...
That you heard "Clarice" play...

Lots of friends and neighbors...
Sat around and sang a song...
Shared the luscious meal and left...
Feeling real stuffed, all night long...

Thank you for all of your talents...
From piano to planning the feast...
Your hard work will not be forgotten...
You're appreciated...to say the least...

Written by Margaret Bergeron
March 17, 1997

HALLOWEEN...

The night is filled with scary things...
Shadows to make us shudder...
No matter how hard you try...
Fright just makes us stutter...

You worry and you wonder...
What's that behind the tree...
Are you only imagining...?
Or will it jump at me...?

Frankenstein or Dracula...
Pirates and Robin Hood...
No matter what your costume...
You know you <u>must</u> look good...

For Halloween is <u>just</u> about fun...
And getting lots of sweets...
Sharing it with your family...
No silly tricks...just treats...

Written by Margaret Bergeron
October 31, 1997

NEW YEAR'S RESOLUTIONS...

Sometimes they last the whole year...
Most times, a month or two...
Maybe just a week at most..
"Resolutions" are hard to do...

You vow to quit your smoking...
You promise not to cheat...
So, instead of smoking cigarettes...
You then begin to eat!!!...

You vow to stop your eating...
By taking diet pills...
Then you're sick from losing weight
And have all kinds of ills...

So then you quit the dieting...
And gain back all the pounds...
You knew that smoking cigarettes...
Kept your weight within its bounds...

Look at a pack of cigarettes...
Then study yourself in the mirror...
It's better to have "A LOT" of you now...
Than to not have a choice in a year...

So, before your "RESOLUTIONS" start...
Make it something you can do...
Start out slow and achieve your goal...
And it won't be so hard on you...

Written by Margaret Bergeron
December 23, 1997

EL NINO

People laughed at weathermen...
The captions and BOLD type...
All the skeptics with their doubts...
Made jokes about the "hype"...

No one ever thought the rain...
Would ever show its face...
Everyone kept close-watch...
For the first drops...and the place...

They said that it was coming...
It even has a name...
"El Nino" didn't sound so bad...
Nevertheless, it came...

All the drains and waterways...
Up and down our coast...
Have held so much, and moves so fast...
Scary to say the most...

Our neighbors to the north of us...
Have surely had their share...
Be assured, we hope that you...
Know how much we care...

Every day brings something new...
And then the sun peeks through...
Always leaving a rainbow...
"God's Promise" to me and you...

So buckle up your rain boots...
Stack sandbags up real well...
Get batteries for your flashlights...
We're in for a real wet spell...!

Written by Margaret Bergeron
February 1998

DO YOU BELIEVE IN SANTA...?

If you believe in Santa...
And all the smiles he brings...
With all the "elves" and North Pole toys...
That the Christmas carolers sing...

If you believe he gobbles up...
All the milk and cookies too...
And slithers down your chimney stack...
Leaving stockings "stuffed" for you...

If you believe his stomach...
Is like a bowl of Jello...
And he's loving, kind and giving...
A real special type of fellow...

Then you have the Christmas spirit...
And you always will believe...
Because, you believing in Santa Claus...
Is whatever you perceive...

Keep the wonder and the awe alive...
It helps to keep us spry...
Besides, we know he's watching...
With that "twinkle" in his eye...

Of course we believe in Santa...
His is real for you and me...
If you stop believing in that jolly man...
"No gifts from him...beneath your tree"...

My parents told me years ago...
Their words I won't forget...
"If you don't believe, you won't receive"...
So, do I believe...? <u>YOU BET</u>...!!!

Written by Margaret Bergeron
December 1997

THE HOUR HAS PASSED

The hour has passed...
So, now is the day...
The year has begun...
What more can we say...?
You made it through New Years...
The world did not end...
You have food and water...
And money to spend...
You have gas in your car...
Your power and phone…
Not afraid of the shortage...
Or of being alone…
The hype and concern...
The anticipation...
Kind of a "let down"…
A bit of frustration...
So save all your excess...
For a flood or a quake...
Or share with your neighbors…
Or use it to bake...
Or, seal it all up...
Store it away...
The world didn't end…
We began a new day...!
You now have a chance...
To make a new start...
Give love to your family...
With all of your heart...

Written by Margaret Bergeron
January 1, 2000

THE FIRST SPRING OF DAY...

On the day that I was born...
My Mother's voice did say...
"Our new little girl was born..."
"On the First Spring of Day...!"

She was so excited by having a girl...
(After two big boys before)...
That saying "The First day of Spring"...
Would, have been a bore...

More than 60 years have passed...
Since that First Spring of Day...
And because today is my birthday...
There's something I want to say...

My parents gave me everything...
For <u>that</u> I am so blest...
God gave me the Mom and Dad...
That truly are the BEST...

And since it is my special, day...
I want to let them know...
That all my words of love and thanks...
IS BECAUSE THEY TAUGHT ME SO...

A child can only learn as much...
As a parent is willing to teach...
Your child can only be hugged and loved...
If they are within your reach...

So, thank you to my Morn and Dad...
I sure love you, and I say...
I'm so glad you had me...
On "THIS FIRST SPRING OF DAY..."

Written by Margaret Bergeron...1999

WHAT ABOUT THE CHILDREN ?

Look at the little children…
Walking around on the street…

Such sad eyes, nowhere to go…
Not trusting people they meet…

Someone, somewhere broke a promise…
To cherish, to teach and to care…

Forgot that being a mom and a dad…
Meant warmth and a home-life to share…

Someone gave up and closed all the doors…
That made it so hard to go on…

Never a thought of the children…
The life of their daughter or son…

Somewhere out there is a child…
That can't understand where you've been…

Not long ago, you gave them your all…
And, now you've abandoned them…

By Margaret Bergeron
March 1997

RETREAT...

Retreat is when you go away...
To find shelter from the storm...
A place to go discover...
Peace in another form...

Retreats can offer refuge...
Or cover up your fears...
A temporary harbor...
For days, or months or years...

Retreat can mean a sanctuary...
A place to take a rest...
Withdrawal from reality...
To heal and feel your best...

Retreat doesn't mean to abandon.
Or leave your life behind...
It's just a thing you've got to do...
So that you won't lose your mind...

Retreat is a "quick" retirement...
A week or just a day...
To take some time to access yourself...
While you're on your "getaway"...

So make a plan to just retreat...
Think of the peace you'll feel...
Sort things out, or just have fun...
Laugh, cry, just be real...

On your return, some things will change...
You'll be calmer than before...
Retreats can make things different...
That's what you take them for...

Written by Margaret Bergeron
April 1998

VETERANS...

We've seen the movies and read the books...Of how it must have been...
But we don't know how it really is...<u>How</u>, could we begin...?

Unless you've lost a loved one...A neighbor, daughter, son...
The grief goes deep inside a heart...Their life, <u>lost</u>...not <u>won</u>...

They are the heroes in our hearts...Many heroes will remain...
Carrying scars and memories...Told and untold pain...

They are the ones that see it all...The ones that keep going on...
The heroes that carry the burden...The misery and the gun...

Could we even fathom...How heavy are their hearts...?
Even now, through all the years...Their vision still imparts...

All the Veterans, everywhere...Deserve a life that's good...
With praises and opportunities...Like all our heroes should...

All the Veterans that you know...Have all been in a scene...
Sitting behind an official desk...In a jungle, or submarine...

Everyone has done their part...From Nurses to Doctors to You...
Keeping up their spirits...Morale and love letters too...

Whether your dear loved one...Was Air Force or Marines...
Army or the Navy...Some were only teens...

Every one a Veteran...They all deserve Salutes...
Respect for what they've done for us...And what it constitutes..

God Bless You, ALL our Veterans...Your families as well...
We may not know exactly...But it must have felt like hell...!
Thank you to all the Veterans everywhere...We DO appreciate you...
And for all the Brave Soldiers serving our Country, even as we speak...

Written by Margaret Bergeron...November 2001

SO MANY AMERICAN SORROWS

So many American sorrows…All over the world as well…
Enemies have "TRIED" to turn our lives…Into a living hell…

We'll always remember Tuesday…Nine/One One/"O" One…
All of those innocent people…Many lives had just begun…

How could anyone do this…?What causes can we find…?
Senseless, horror and destruction…Are forever on our mind…

All the loved ones that have vanished…Trapped or gone, this day…
Workers, Firemen, Police, MD's…For ALL the people…PRAY…

Such a tremendous loss in lives…Normal people, doing their job…
Going to work in the morning…But, by noon, their *families were robbed*…

How do we thank our Country…?
Helpers, neighbors, friends…
The ones that are out there still working…Until the last day will end…

The "innocent" on airplanes were helpless…
To the wickedness, and the distain…
They had no way out, no good choices…Can't
imagine, their families…their pain…

Our President has a long journey…He needs
ALL our prayers and our thoughts…
All of us pulling TOGETHER…Show love for the ones who CANNOT…

"They've" put some pits in America…Not the <u>SPIRIT</u> of our World…
"They've" tried to pull it all apart…But we CANNOT be unfurled…!

Please, God, let YOUR world join together…
Punish those, who *mean* to do harm…
Hold all your faithful in the Palm of Your Hand…
The "uncertain" to lean on YOUR ARM…

Written by Margaret Bergeron
September 11, 2001

IF WE ALL LOOKED THE SAME...

Does it really matter...
The color of our skin...
If we're all the same shade...
Would love and peace begin...?

Would the gangs and racists...
Stop all the drugs and wars...
Would the drive-by shootings...
Stop threatening our doors...?

Would the schools and colleges...
Choose merit on its own...?
Would a house be opened up...
Offer everyone a loan...?

Would you be any less afraid...?
Of walking down the street...
Would you be any friendlier...?
To people that you meet...?

If our language and accents...
Sounded exactly like each other...
Would we start embracing life...?
Being like sisters and brothers...?

Would the world start changing...?
If we all looked the same...?
If we saw no difference...
Who would there be to blame...?

If only we could strive to do...
The very best we can....
To try to make some changes...
To make a life long plan...

Written by Margaret Bergeron
January 1999

WHY ARE THERE BAD PEOPLE...?

Why doesn't "EVERYONE" want peace...?
Why are there "so many BAD"...?
There's room in this world for "ALL" of us...
We're not supposed to be so sad...
Why do some try to scare us...?
Still others want to do harm...
Making another suffer so...
While causing so much alarm...

Trying to make it difficult....
To even get through the day...
Instead of showing love and care...
They choose the "other" way...
A very sad part, in all of this...
Are the innocent peoples' "fright"...
Why can't the BAD "just fight with each other"...?
Then this could work out just right...

We live in a beautiful Country...
Where we felt safe, we were free...
To open our mail and fly in the skies...
Take the train, or the bus, sail the sea...
Where water and food are plentiful...
And children could "trick or treat"...
Washing your hands was something you did...
Before you just sat down to eat...

Looking at all of the buildings...
So tall and so carefully planned...
How sad that we can't still be carefree...
Fear has permeated our laud…
There's one thing that CANNOT he taken...
No matter how "bad people" may try...
"Bad people" can't take GOD, out of our hearts...
"Bad people"… don't even know why...!

Written By Margaret Bergeron
September 11, 2001

ABOUT OUR SKY...

Have you ever thought about...
The sky and what it holds...
How you can depend on light...
As well as dark or cold...
How all the clouds make forms...
Making way for wind or rain...
And how a rainbow then shows up...
When it is calm again...
How the sky gets angry...
With rods of fiery light...
And thunder makes its presence...
Throughout a stormy night...
How the sun gets brighter...
As summer time gets nigh...
And how it cools in winter...
Letting snow float from the sky...
How the hail can form to last...
Do you ever wonder why...?
How dark turns to light so fast...
When the sun is in our sky...
And how the moon knows when to shine...
Or to show us...just a part...
Of our moon's shining glory...
That touches romantic hearts...
How our moon and our warm sun...
Can change our ocean's tide...
How the tide can change the sea...
Where all the fish reside...
And most of all, how it all works...
How wondrous, the sky of blue...
How looking up and praying...
Is something we just do...
We know that God is everywhere...
Though, we look to heaven to pray...
Our sky is overwhelming...
Every night and every day...

Written by Margaret Bergeron.
March 21, 2000

A MISGIVING...

A misgiving could be anything...
That we don't use too well...
It could be a physical or mental thing...
Even very hard to tell...

Could be beauty or homely...
Handsome as well as plain...
Money just as penniless...
Good health as well as pain...

Fancy job or welfare...
It's all what you perceive...
The amount of money won't matter...
It's the trail that your life will leave...

Other's misgivings can make us sigh...
Yet, our faults should make us groan...
We get so involved in other's lives...
We forget about fixing our own...

Concentrate on good traits...
Not on just the bad...
You'd be surprised how friendships bloom...
(Even improve the ones you've had!)...

What ever you think a misgiving is...
Believe the words I say...
"The words that you speak about others...
Will come back to you someday"...

Written by Margaret Bergeron...1996

TOMORROW NEVER SHOWS

When you worry 'bout tomorrow...
You see, it never shows...
Cause by the time it should arrive...
To the next day, it goes...

You wonder and you ponder...
What will tomorrow be...?
You forget the beauty of today...
And the wonders you could see...

You'll never find "tomorrow"...
(Wonder where that word was made?)...
(Someone wishing their days away)...
(Just lying in the shade?)...

Forget about "Tomorrow"...
It won't come anyway...
You'll waste your time, and you will see...
It goes into "yesterday"...

Tomorrow is a "worry" word...
It only clouds your way...
Taking grace and blessings...
Meant for you "this day"...

Today is here, so take it...
Use every single minute...
Forget about tomorrow...
There is no future in it...

Written by Margaret Bergeron
July 1999

FEELING A BIT LOW...?

If you're feeling a bit low...
You find it hard to smile...
If you feel you want to cry...
More than once in awhile...
If you feel like sleeping...
Or sitting through the day...
Don't even feel like talking...
You have nothing much to say...

Don't know how long you'll feel like this...
Can't help it, you just do...
It will probably pass in time...
You'll get back to being you...

So many things are happening...
It's not our "usual" world...
Terrorists have "tried" to change...
But don't let our lives unfurl...

We all are feeling a bit low...
And maybe it's hard to smile...
Your tears will "probably" still fall...
But less, after awhile...

When you wake up each morning...
Before you even rise...
Ask Our Lord to fill your day...
With Faith...He'll dry your eyes...

Written By Margaret Bergeron
2000

BEING AFRAID...

What are you afraid of...?Is it something you should fear...?
Did the fear start recently...?Has it lingered through the years...?
Are you like so many...?Who tremble in the dark...?
Are you afraid of rain or floods...?Or shadows in the park...?

Are you afraid of driving...?Along our crowded streets...?
Going into shopping malls...?Or a stranger you might meet...?
Maybe you are afraid of dogs...?Or even worse, of snakes...?
Just the very sight of them...Is sometimes all it takes...

Hurricanes or a tornado...Blizzard or an earthquake...
Everyone dreads all of these...And a fear can make you shake...
Some are afraid of being locked in...A few cannot breathe in a crowd...
Most are afraid of being alone...Or cover their ears from things loud...

Fears are things that you can create..."Times" you feel most insecure...
You try to make them disappear...You'd like to succeed, that's for sure...
Never laugh at somebody's fears...Its a very serious matter...
Fear can freeze you to the bone...Making all confidence shatter...

One day that fear will go away...You'll hardly remember when....
You'll be free from that one...And another one will begin...!!

Written by Margaret Bergeron
February 1998

56

LORD, FILL MY TANK...

Lord, help me to remember...
And thank you for each day...
For all that you have given me...
(And sometimes, take away...)
For breezes blowing through my hair...

On days that I can't bear...
For reminding me that You won't leave...
You're here and everywhere...
For people riding next to me...

For those who need to know...
That when my tank feels empty...
You're filling it up, real slow...
You're with me when I take each breath...
When I close my eyes to sleep...
And when I wake up frightened...
When I Pray, "My soul, You'll keep"...
And when I'm laughing, smiling too...

Or, when my tears fill up my eyes...
Remind me how You've filled my tank...
On all those days gone by...
Those days I've been on empty...

When I thought, "I can't go on..."
Despair and sadness came around...
But You just said, "Be gone"...
Lord, help to fill my tank each day...

With everything I need...
Remind me that You're watching...
So Your rules, I sure will heed...
And when I feel my tank is low...

Please get me to the place...
That I can call upon Your name...
Please, let me see Your face...
And, when my time on earth is done...

My last ride will start towards You...
"Fill my tank, Lord"... bring me Home...
<u>Only You</u> can guide me through...

Written by Margaret Bergeron

SEASONS OF OUR LIVES...

There are many, many seasons...That we travel through each year...
Not only the "four" seasons...Am I speaking of right here...
Of course, we have the Winter...Summer, Spring and Fall...
We can just about predict...When they begin to call...
What I am referring to...And what I bring to mind...
Are the "Seasons" that we all go through...
(We can't "choose" them, you will find...)
Seasons of your life, are those...That come when not prepared...
Sometimes leave us happy...Confident or scared...
Seasons of great "Loss" can come...Or, Seasons of "Plenty and Giving"...
There are Seasons of "Hardship"...(When you can barely make a living)...
Then, there are the "Smooth" times...When things cannot go wrong...
Life feels perfect and loving...Like singing a happy song...
You forget to ready yourself...For "Other" Seasons of your life...
Taking "Plenty" and "Great" for granted...Then along comes "Strife"...
"Strife" is a woeful Season...That takes your breath away...
'Til the Season of "Love" appears...Bringing a brand new day...
Where do you go in "Lonely" times...?Do you just throw up your hands...?
Or do you cling to Faith in God...(The only One who understands)...
If you wait 'til a "Season of Loss"...To start Praying to find a "Reason"...
You won't have the "strongest" strength...
To get through that difficult Season...
Put your life in the One who cares...Guides you and you can trust...
No matter, in good or rough times...Surely, you know, that you must...
Seasons come and Seasons go...Each one another stage...
Documenting each Season of Life...Saving memories as we age...
Embrace the "Seasons of your Life"...Each one has a place that we share...
Seasons of "Plenty" are easy and light...Seasons of Loss...take your air...
We can get through all these Seasons...Enjoy all the days of your life...
Seasons of Loving and Giving...Outweigh all the Seasons of Strife...
So where you are today, is not...Where you'll be tomorrow...
Today you may be lonely...Tomorrow, no more sorrow...
Remember that no matter what...Or how or when or where...
IF you are going through Seasons with "God"...He'll "hold you" through
each one with care...

Written by Margaret Bergeron
2005

LETTER TO OPRAH

I've longed to write this letter...I've waited for so long...
Putting off my fears, and now...I hope that I'm not wrong...
I've been writing many years...Since I was only ten...
Words just rhyme inside my head...And, that's where I'll begin...
Never known who I could trust...With poetry I've done...
You're such a caring person...My confidence you've won...
I'd love to write some poetry...In your Magazine called "O"...
"Wander With Me" by Margaret...It's the name that suits me so.

I'm writing for a newspaper..."The Mobile Homeowner News"...
Every week I write a poem...Makes you smile and cures the blues...
Twelve years of being published there...Volunteering all my time...
Getting much appreciation...For all my written rhymes...
When I see your Book Club...I've dreamed, "It could be me"...
Holding up my heartfelt words...For all the world to see...
I've been so encouraged...And, I would like to be...
Part of what you stand for...You, Oprah Winfrey...!

You've given me the courage...In ways you cannot see...
You're someone I admire so...For what you've come to be...
My dream has always been the same...My gift is God's Own Giving...
My Family and Friends a bonus...Not finer ingredients for living...
Married my high school Sweetheart...He's the apple of my eye...
He's been my hero 42 years...He's really a wonderful guy...
I can write a rhyming poem...Any subject that you choose...
Friendship, love and memories...Or to chase away the blues...

A poem about a person...A place or an event...
About a special birthday...Where a holiday is spent...
If you have some great ideas...Or know where I can start...
I'd sure do my very best...And work with all my heart...
Thanks for all you do for us...You've made a difference here...
You always go that extra mile...You're blessed and very dear...
Oprah, I have shared a bit...Of what I'd like to do...
Enclosed, some of my poetry...I'll leave the rest to you...

Written by Margaret Bergeron
July 24, 2000

KATRINA...

No one knows why this happened...
Such a devastating day...
The force of water, wind and rain...
Hit our U. S. of A....!
The news reports are oh, so sad...
The pictures make us cry...
They're living such a nightmare...
So many had to die...
We pray for all the many lives...
That Katrina took for sure...
Let's not forget to pray for those...
Whose homes were on the shore...
They need so much from all of us...
To get back on their feet...
The little things like blankets...
Water and food to eat...

So if you think about it...
If you want to do some good...
Help in any way you can...
We all know that we should...
It could be any one of us...
When disaster shows its face...
Think of the comforts that we have...
And what could take its place...
Now its time to come together...
All religions, race and creeds...
Right now our nation begs for help...
They have so many needs...
So put aside some time today...
Dig deep and you will see...
That a "little" is a "lot" to most...
They have less than you and me...
And keep in mind the things you do...
Will make you smile and say...
"Someone will get help from me"...
It will brighten both your days...

Written by Margaret Bergeron...August 2005

FORGIVENESS...

We're told by God, "We must forgive"…
Even though it's very hard…
'Cause it applies to everyone…
Not just those in our front yard…
Our loved ones may have wronged us…
Many years ago…
Forgiving is a command from God…
The Bible tells us so…
If you are holding grudges…
Keeping you from letting go…
Not allowing healing…
Not forgiving, saying, "No"…
Think of what our Savior did…
For us…just to forgive…
He gave His life for those He loved…
Therefore, we all can live…
You know, it hurts to drop that grudge…
Felt better to hold it tight…
Made it easier to point the blame…
Than to forgive and sleep at night…
Each day, you decide "not" to forgive…
You harbor anger in your heart…
You turn your face away from God…
Each day, right from the start…
If your day starts with forgiveness…
It is time that you can spend…
Pushing all that anger out…
From beginning to the end…

Written By Margaret Bergeron…2001

A DIFFICULT SEASON...

Every time you're angry...or...
In a difficult "Season"...
Remember, God is by your side...
You're "in it" for a reason...

You've maybe had a "bad day"...
So sorry you're so sad...
Perhaps a dose of "friendship"...
Won't make it seem so bad...

Sometimes some things "just happen"...
We can't "just" have it good...
Or we couldn't learn life's lessons...
Like we know we should...

There's always something "worse" that could...
Take over something "little"...
Please be glad that you are blessed...
With a choice "nearest the middle"...

You're passing a "really hard" time...
It's one of those "Difficult Seasons"...
The next one could be filled with joy...
For, "unexplainable" reasons...

So thank "Our Lord" for all your joys...
But especially for the bad...
Cause "HE'S ALWAYS STANDING NEXT TO US"
So, today, please don't be sad...

Written by Margaret Bergeron
January 2006

62

WHERE DO YOU GO...

Where do you go to get away...From what encircles you...
Whether it is just everyday life...Or the regular job that you do...

So many places to be alone...(But getting there is the key)...
You start out in one direction...Its destination you never see...

Some head straight to the mountains...With a cool fresh hilltop view...
Some go to the desert to bake...Where the heat sure gets to you...

Others go to lakes and streams...To fish or boat or ski...
Some climb cliffs or rocky points...To relax...to some degree...

But take me to the ocean...For waves and sand and sun...
Let the tide be high or low...That's where I find my fun...

You see some riding surfboards...Or fins and boogie board...
I like sitting upon the sand...Not saying a single word...

There's something special about the beach...That can quiet anyone...
Listening to the seagulls...Watch the waves...While feeling the sun...

No one can capture the fury of waves...Not canvas, nor photo, or pen...
Unless you are sitting and feeling the sand...Then you really will begin...

Because the way that the waves are breaking...Sun and shells and sand...
The birds and breeze and surfers...Combining them is, so grand...

Written by Margaret Bergeron
October 1997

WHAT IS LOVE...

Some say it is the warmth you feel...
When you wake in the middle of night...
Some say it is a glow...When he holds you tight...

Some say it's a letter...When he's far away...
Some say it's the way...That he calls every day...

Some say it's him...When a good thing he's done...
Some say it's everything...Wrapped up into one...

Love brings may gifts...To real hearts in love..
Some say that these gifts...Are sent from above...

Happiness, Faith...And Charity too...
Could surely prove...That your love was true...

Eyes that meet...From across a dance...
Might even lead...To real romance...

Some say that love...Makes everything work out...
Love is just wonderful...To that there's no doubt...!

Written by Margaret "McClinton" Bergeron
July 1965

MAN OF THE HOUSE...

To be the man about the house...
What is it you must do...?
All the chores requiring strength...
And help with dishes too...
You usually get the paper...
Squash the bug at night...
Open up the tightened jar...
Replace the kitchen light...
Pull the toughest weeds...
Change oil in the truck...
Teach the children how to drive...
Take over when they are stuck...
Teach the morals in the home...
Be strong when we are weak...
Know the words we need to hear...
When we feel too sad to speak...
Compliments for everything...
Massage our feet at night...
We'll cook and clean and organize...
You know how to treat us right...
You men sure are important...
There is no room for fibs...
You got us for companions...
And we stole one of your ribs...
This poem is written just for you...
Dads and men everywhere...
Because you carry the heavier load...
To let us know you care...
You are the man about the house...
But only a day set aside...?
Seems like you guys got slighted.
You deserve a longer ride...

Written By Margaret Bergeron...2004

REMEMBER THAT I LOVE YOU…

Remember that I love you…
As you wander off today…
Remember that I care for you…
No matter what you say…

Remember that a Mother's job…
Is harder than you suppose…
Much more than teaching manners…
Or blotting a runny nose…

It's more than doing homework…
Or teaching you to eat…
It's more about life's lessons…
And where to plant your feet…

It's teaching you about your needs…
From a mother's point of view…
It's helping you to sort out the junk…
You think life has dealt to you…

It's just because I love you so…
That I feel so insecure…
About the way you live your life…
You seem a bit unsure…

Respecting yourself and your family…
Means so much when you're a mother…
Remember that I love you so…
And you're special like no other…

Written by Margaret Bergeron
February 1998

THE JOURNEY

Don't be so focused on the future…
That you forget to enjoy the ride…
Keep your eyes wide open…
With your loved ones by your side…

If you look too far ahead…
Just think what you might miss…
The best part is the journey…
Like the warmth before a kiss…

The road is never "always" smooth…
There's lots of bumps and slips…
But, oh how grand the flat roads feel…
Compared to all the dips…

Sometimes we worry way too much…
Like we forget the dreams…
Or why we planned the journey…
Was camouflaged, it seems…

Try to keep your heart so full…
Of love and faith and hope…
That each day just gets better…
Don't sit around and mope…

So focus on the journey…
Not a faraway distraction…
Have some fun just getting there…
Don't miss all the action…

Written by Margaret Bergeron
July 2009

HAVE YOU SAID "I LOVE YOU"...?

Have you said "I love you'...To your love today...
Have you remembered saying "thank you"...For all they do or say...?

Can you recall the little things...It takes to make them smile...
Not even thinking of yourself...Just "ponder" on them awhile...

Little acts of kindness...To brighten up their week...
Say you really appreciate...Each loving word they speak...

Going out of your own way...To make them feel secure...
Giving special hugs and pats...Show you care for sure...!

Trying little special ways...To make your romance fun...
Leaving love notes on the sink...That..."They are Number One"...

Put toothpaste on their toothbrush...Pick a flower. Just because...
Change the mood, and will it work...?It really, truly does...

Only one way to find out...If all this "mush" is true...
Be the one to make the change...And love will shine on you...

We always want our mate to be...A certain way, and yet...
We should be "that certain way"...By giving love, we get...

This is a special week for love...Do something with all your heart...
You'll be surprised with the reply...It could be a brand new start...

Written by Margaret Bergeron
February 1998

MY OLD TORN UP BOOK...

I'm still around...I made it through...
It's been many years...Since I wrote in you...

I read you tonight...You choked me to tears...
So much hurt...For so many years...

I never would guess that so long ago...My life would straighten out...
I was truly so confused...What was it all about...?

I finally found my own true love...Right in the reach of me....
It was my "Billy" after all... It just took time to see...

So now my book can be filled up...With lots of happy things...
Of ups and downs and in and outs...That a sturdy marriage brings...

Written by Margaret Bergeron
August 1983

HANDS OF A LADY...

Smooth as if velvet...For all that they do...
Her hands are the softest...To ever soothe you...

Her hands, like her skin...Slightly weathered and worn...
From the years of the care...Ever since you were born...

All the diapers and clothes...She has changed through the day...
Her hands touched a million...Or more, I would say...

Oh, the tears she has kissed...And the hair she has brushed...
Or the times we didn't need her...She must have been crushed...

The meals she has cooked...With loving hands each day...
The way that she sings...Putting dishes away...

The presents she wraps...Puts the bow on just right...
The card on the top...Inside, "Love", she will write...

She says "no problem", (no matter how hard)...
She does the task with care...
So if she needs a helping hand...Why is "nobody" there...?

We take her hands for granted...Not meaning to, but do...
For no one in this world can touch...That gentle heart like you...

She gets a little slower now...Her eyesight, not the best...
But when you go to see her...She hugs you to her chest...

Nothing can mean more to her...Than gathering her clan...
Watching as they grow up...Holding their little hands...

Her hands have held us all so dear...Warm and healing to the touch...
No wonder that we'd like to thank...The Lady we love so much...

Written By Margaret Bergeron -
May 2002

CROOKED HANDS...

When my hands are not so smooth...
When lines have claimed my face...
When my eyes are not as bright...
Or my feet can't keep the pace...

When my hearing isn't good...
Or I seem slower than heck...
Will you still hold my crooked hands...
And kiss my wrinkled neck...?

Inside we still are teenagers...
Our hearts are still entwined...
We've loved each other longer...
Than a good aged bottle of wine...

No one else could know our hearts...
As we shuffle down the hall...
We've seen just about everything...
We've darn-near heard it all...

Just because our minds get slow...
And we repeat a thing or two...
When our hands get old and crooked...
I'll still be in love with you...

And, if one must go before we wake...
We each will save a part...
One special spot in heaven...
Another in our hearts...

Written by Margaret Bergeron
March 2000

I ONLY HELPED HER CRY...

Someone hurt my friend today...
I never will know why...
I only know, I will be there...
Just to help her cry...

She is such a good friend...
She didn't deserve a lie...
Her gentle heart is hurting so...
I only helped her cry...

His mean deceit by hiding...
The truth for all these years...
I tried to help her out, but I...
Could only wipe her tears...

Trust is something given...
When we deserve it, by...
Proving we are worthy...
It hurts to see her cry...

Time will pass and hurt will fade...
Although we continue to sigh...
God will help to mend her heart...
I could only help her cry...

Written by Margaret Bergeron
November 1998

THE ROAD...

The road won't always be rocky...The road will <u>rarely</u> be smooth...
The road that you will travel on...May calm or sting or soothe…

It sometimes will be bumpy...And mostly be uphill...
The downhill times are wonderful...<u>Relish</u> the peaceful and still…

You may stumble on a gloomy path...With flickering rays of light...
A little on the scary side...(If you don't walk just right)...

It can take a turn near crossroads…And you will have to choose...
Which road to take...which one to leave...What have you got to lose…?

<u>Only</u> your direction...In choosing right from wrong…
<u>Then</u> the road is simple…<u>RIGHT</u> directions don't take too long...

But if you fret and worry so...And lose your sleep at night...
Not knowing where to make a turn...Then you <u>KNOW</u> it can't be right…

Which ever road or path you take...Keep one <u>MAIN</u> thing in mind...
You'll pass and touch a lot of lives...Remember to be kind...

Because you never know just how...Your <u>WORDS</u> may change the road...
Of someone who is <u>NEEDING</u> care...Or carries a "HEAVIER" load…..

Written by Margaret Bergeron
January 1998

GENERATIONS OF TREES...

Look at the trees in a forest...Or alongside a mountain so tall...
Think of them all as a family...Each one, representing us all...

The Big ones are older and wiser...Stronger and limbs guarding all...
Giving some shade to the young ones below...
And relief to the ones not so tall...

Look closer and you will see sad ones...Whose limbs are all straggly and slim...
Maybe a tree did not get enough food...Or some kind of disease got to him...

Some trees are shorter and fatter...Some are so different and marred...
Some just have half of their branches...Where fire has left them so scarred...

Some give us shade in the morning...Some are all brown from decay...
Others have fallen and cannot get up...So that is just where they will lay...

The trees that are strong and are healthy...House
squirrels and birds in their trunks...
Kind of like families with children...With houses and bedrooms with bunks...

All throughout the whole forest...With hundreds and hundreds of trees...
Every one different in stature...Each one free to do as they please...

How very much like our families...Are forests of trees, great and strong...
Some never have a care in the world...Some living right, some live wrong...

One tree leans over, is weeping...The grove of her trees in a mess...
Much like the weeping of mothers...When he hurt of a child they confess...

Each time you stand in a forest...Or think of the trees near your home...
Remember the difference in families...And
how separate branches must roam...

One thing about trees in the forest...No matter how big or diseased...
Unless they are cut up for firewood...None of them gets up and leaves...

Generations of trees in the forest...Like miracles, Gods own design...
Could not match the beauty and wonder...He gave to your family and mine...

Written By Margaret Bergeron
July 2001

74

LIFE MINUS LOVE = NOTHING...

You may think you don't have a purpose...
That life is just that and no more...
That whatever happens, just happens...
With no meaning, way down to the core...

Life without love equals nothing...
Just emptiness, nothing to hold...
No real connection to friendships...
Makes you feel lonely and cold...

Fill up your heart with "love's softness"...
Let all of that happiness in...
Promise yourself to be gentle and kind...
Then watch as the love filters in...

Give to yourself, some patience...
Mixed in with a little remorse...
Forgive "yourself" and then, "others"...
Then watch as your life changes course...

People will look at you different...
With amazement and a raise of their brow...
Taking interest, you'll change your whole outlook...
You'll feel LIFE and your LOVE will show now...

But if you take love away from your life...
It's boring and bland without smiles...
There's no substitute for God's precious gift...
It's been waiting for you all the while...

Written By Margaret Bergeron
September 2001

75

A ROSE WITH NO THORNS...

A life that has no obstacles...
A life that has no pain...
Can hardly be contented...
What would there be to gain...?

A little bit of sadness...
A tiny smidgen of grief....
Would surely make the great times shine...
And offer some relief...

Until you know the hurts in life...
You cannot feel the bliss...
Until you've loved another...
What good would be a kiss...?

The thorn upon a roses stem...
Can hurt your finger...yet...
The fragrance from the roses scent...
Is one you won't forget...

A rose that has no thorns on it...
Is said, "cannot be sweet"...
Just try one from your garden...
Bought ones can't compete...

Not to say, a store bought rose...
Can't thrill you to no end...
It's always in "the thought that counts"...
And the message that it sends...

Every rosebud has its own way...
Of making beauty show...
How ever did God make them...?
How does He make them grow...?
(Someday, He'll let us know)...

Written by Margaret Bergeron
December 1997

PICKED A ROSE...

I picked a rose this morning...
Hoping it would make me smile…
Someone hurt my feelings...
To mend, may take a while…

The rose's fragrance lifted me…
Its leaves are darkest green...
A neighbor took my hand and smiled…
Best medicine I've seen...

Life is sometimes less than great...
But... who said it would be…?
Trying to find a place, where...
Idle words won't bother me...

Today I "took" a moment…
Looked at a rose to see...
Although the thorns are vicious…
Its beauty captured me...

It didn't take the hurt away...
Although it made me pray...
For the one that hurt my feelings...
And made me feel this way...

Written by Margaret Bergeron
August 4, 1998

LOOK AT A ROSE…

Pick a rosebud from the garden…
Watch it open up each day…
The petals will carefully unfold…
In a most romantic way…

A rose can brighten any home…
Just try and you will see..
Placing a rose in every room…
Will relax you, I guarantee…

Something is mellow about a rose…
It beauty, scent and feel..
The way it changes by the hour…
Almost seems unreal…

I've heard that God's Own Signature…
Is placed on the rose's stem…
He surely chose the perfect way…
To have us think of Him…

When you've finished reading this…
I tell you what to do…
Pick a rose and look at it…
And say, "thank you" that it grew…

Because a single rosebud…
Picked by hand with love…
Is grander than a dozen "bought"…
'Cause it's picked with a garden glove…

Written by Margaret Bergeron
September 1997

IF YOU ONLY KNEW...

If you only knew today...What tomorrow's day would bring...
You would spend your whole life...Being stressed about each thing...

You probably wouldn't even sleep...So keyed up, you would be...
No one would come near you...'Cause, the future's not ours to see...

That's why "living for today"...Is what we're told to do...
This way no one knows for sure...What's happening to you...

If you only knew today...Tomorrow's day "on cue"...
No one would even have to say..."Hello and how are you..."

Everyone would know the news...You wouldn't have to read...
Not even watch the newscast...Or what ball team will lead...

You'd know if you had passed a test...Before you even took it...
You'd know you felt an earthquake...Before the earth had "Shook it"...

You'd know ahead of time, just how…A story would start and end...
And what would be the price to pay…?
We could never "Just wonder" again...

So, next time you want to know...What's happening tomorrow...
Be glad you do not know for sure...It could be joy or sorrow...

Just live each day completely…In all you do and say...
Don't worry about tomorrow...It won't help you in any way...

Written by Margaret Bergeron
February 1998

ONCE YOU KNEW SOMEBODY...

Once you knew somebody...
Always made you grin...
Think way back, remember...?
I'll let <u>you</u> fill in...

Always saw the best in friends...
Treating all with care...
Seeing only good in life...
Remember, being there..?

Energy abounding...
Running to and fro...
Never out of things to try...
Where did that someone go...?

Got up before the chickens...
To exercise and bake...
Plan a fun activity...
Then off to frost a cake...

Never thought a selfish thought...
Would never think to cuss...
Nothing bothersome or rude...
Never made a fuss...

It may be coincidence...
May be someone you knew...
Wouldn't it be something, if...
That "Somebody" is you...?

Written By Margaret Bergeron
July 2000

LITTLE "MELODEE"...

A tiny feathered hummingbird...
At the top of one bare tree...
No other birds around her...
She's just looking at you and me...

The music plays while we all swim...
Then Melodee will prance...
Flits away but comes right back...
She opens her wings to dance...

She is our special little bird...
She's musical, you should see...
Above the pool, she dives and darts...
Our little Melodee...

Each day she's sitting up there...
Like she can hardly wait...
To hear the music and the sounds...
She truly can relate...

She waits each day, our feathered friend...
Her beak so long and slim...
She is our private audience...
While we're in the pool to swim...

Other birds pay us no mind...
They do not dance or sway...
Only our little Melodee...
Comes to visit us each day...

Written by Margaret Bergeron
March 2004

81

ON THE EDGE OF THE SHORE...

Watching the water...
Through all the trees...
Sun going down...
Feeling the breeze...

Green eyes are staring...
Hidden so well...
Silently Waiting...
No one could tell...

What should she do...
She's feeling so sad...
On the edge of the shore...
What could be so bad...

Bigger green eyes...
From the forest nearby...
Feeling her pain...
Watching her cry...

No where to turn...
The day slowly ends...
The sun reappears...
A new day begins...

Written by Margaret Bergeron
September 2000

BE CAREFUL WHAT YOU WISH FOR...

Don't wish he'd stop his snoring...
Or she'd stop shopping at the mall...
Or that he wouldn't golf so much...
Or play Bingo at the hall...

Or to do the dishes better...
Not play with the remote...
Not to tell you what to do...
(Especially "how" to vote)...

Not to drive so slow or fast...
Or choose just where to eat...
Don't wish for peace or quiet...
Or for a lone retreat...

Think of all the little things...
You wish for every day...
Things you'd miss so "awfully much!"...
If they ever went away...

You see, you never think that it...
Really could be true...
What ever it is you wish for...
Could happen....to you...

Written By Margaret Bergeron
March 2001

A HITCH IN YOUR GIT-ALONG...

Does it mean you're tuckered out...
Or that you have the flu....?
Maybe just a little pain...
Or a broken "Thing a magoo"...

Possibly a cold or cough...
Or a nagging head that aches...
A good, hot tasty, chicken soup...
With some crackers you could make...

Maybe it's arthritis...
A joint that creaks and cracks...
Maybe its your neck or hands...
Or, some pressure in your back...

Some days, you feel wonderful...
Other days it's bad...
Mostly more UP than DOWN...
For that, you sure are glad...

There are liniments for achy bones...
Pills to ease the pain...
Vitamins for energy...
Or stiff joints, from the rain...

Whatever it is that ails you...
And, a most familiar phrase...
You've got hitch in your git along"...
That's got you down these days...!

Written by Margaret Bergeron
February 2000

BEING BLUE...

Everyone goes through those days...
That take away your smile...
Make you sad and woeful...
Can last for quite a while...

You wake up with a frown on...
The tears appear as well...
Your mood is such a mystery...
Last night, you felt swell...

Wandering about your house...
Like you're not even there...
Nothing really wrong with you...
And, you don't even care...

If asked "why are you crying?"...
You cannot even tell...
Nothing hurts, nothing aches...
You just can't control the well...

Maybe you are tired...
Though, you slept real sound last night...
Maybe you are just worn out...
Or, perhaps, a bit uptight...

Maybe you just need a break...
Take off a day or two...
Maybe it is normal...
Just a day of <u>Being Blue...</u>

Doesn't mean you need a pill...
Or that you're going crazy...
Probably all you really need...
Is a day to just be lazy...

Written by Margaret Bergeron
October 1999

IF WE GREW "DOWN" INSTEAD OF "UP"...

If we started out as seniors...And ended up as tots...
Think of how much fun we'd have...We'd know an awfully lot...

We'd be so full of knowledge...We'd be brilliant from the start...
Our health would just improve each day...And so would our "old" hearts...

We'd know which way was best to go...And where we'd want to live...
We'd be full of excitement...We'd have so much time to give...

We need not plan our "future"...We'd be going "down" the ladder...
We'd live each day so anxiously...Time, just wouldn't matter...

Our jobs would be so different...We'd get younger every day...
Instead of being so tuckered out...We'd have brand, new things to say...

We'd look "back" at our pictures...See wrinkles disappear...
Our hair would gradually get less gray...The "bald"...hair would reappear...

Our sight would just get better...Throw those spectacles away...
We'd gradually lose age spots...Sit in the sun for one whole day...

Our aging skin would tighten up...We'd feel our muscles pull...
Eating ice cream late at night...Would be a new found rule...

We'd love getting up real early...We'd not want to miss a minute...
Growing "down" instead of "up"...Would have "adventure" in it...

Written by Margaret Bergeron
February 1999

WHERE WE'RE NEEDED...

We never know where we're needed...
From day to day we go...
About our normal business...
Where we're needed, we don't know...
You could be in the right place...
At just the perfect time...
About to leave, but changed your mind...
No reason and no rhyme...

You could be in your car or boat...
Or surfing in a wave...
When you hear a cry for help...
A life, you may just save...
Ever wonder...why it is...
You leave a minute late...?
Then you see an accident...
That could have been <u>your</u> fate...

A day can start so perfectly...
For one about to see...
But sometimes, it ends tragically...
But not today, for me...
The moral to this story...
If, there is one to write...is...
Love your family and pray for them...
Each day and every night...

Never let a day go by...
Without a gentle touch...
Let your loved ones <u>feel</u> your care...
That you love them very much...
We never know where we're needed...
So always be aware...
Some day, someone might need your help...
A life you could help spare...

Written By Margaret Bergeron
April 2002

WHAT WOULD BE...

What would be your last words...?
If you found you could not talk...?
Where would be your final stroll...?
If you found you could not walk...?

What would your eyes gaze upon...?
Should they dim or lose their sight...?
Would you remember light of day...?
Or the beauty from moonlight...?

Should your mind begin to lose...
It's sharpness of memory...
What one thought would you cling to...?
That only you could see...?

And if those hands, so active now...
Should someday lose their hold...
Whose hand would you like to caress...?
As you are growing old...?

Perhaps you think that wondering...
What you would do or say...
Would be a waste of time or thought...
That there's no room in your day...

Just think of how important...
Your words, your mind, your eyes...
Your legs and hands, those comfy hugs...
A friend or a loved one's sigh...

It will help you to remember...
Each day to form your thoughts...
So that what you do each day remains...
To giving all you've got...

Written by Margaret Bergeron
September 1997

ME, MYSELF AND I...

My dear old name is Maggie...
I was born in the U.S.A....
I came to California...
On a bright and sunny day...
I have, I guess some brothers...
But if you're interested in me...
My hair is blonde, my eyes are brown...
I'm awful sight to see...
My favorite singer is Mathis...
To dreamland he takes me...
My actor was Mr. Gable...
But God took him, so you see...
"_____ _____" is my favorite boyfriend...
Fill out the line above...
And I don't think that I'm too young...
To really fall in love...
(1965)
I wouldn't tell-my age to you...
I think I'll make you guess...
In ten years I'll be twenty eight...
But now I'm a little less...
I not so thin and not so fat...
A bit chubby I would say....
But since I'm on a diet...
I get thinner every day...
I go to C.V, High School...
I'm in my senior year...
I love it very dearly...
Now don't you think that's queer...
I love to play the piano...
I love to dance as well...
As for the Lettermen's albums...
I think they are just swell...
I guess I've told my life to you...
And now you know it all...
I hope to see you sometime soon...
Just walking down the hall...

Written by Margaret "McClinton" Bergeron
1959

89

MOTHER'S CHILD...

When your child is finally grown...
And moves so far away...
Most days you just feel the same...
Except on their "Birth" day...
For, their special day is...
Oh, so dear to you...
You share their joy and happy times...
But also when they're blue...

When they have a problem...
No matter, big or small...
Because you are the "Mother"...
They give them to you...ALL...
Mothers, Aunts and Grandmas...
A child goes to your heart...
No matter how hard you try to resist...
Some things you CAN'T pull apart...

Your thoughts are daily drifting...
To your children, far or near...
But, somehow on their Birthday...
The memories ring in your ear...
All of the things they've done, (or do)...
(Mostly good things come to mind)...
The little gestures that made you smile...
The childhood woes left behind...

Special "bonds" on their Birthdays...
You are happy, though sometimes you ache...
They are all grown up...but so far away...
Blowing candles on their Birthday cake...
The feelings never seem to fade...
Mother's love, is forever true...
Your child may move out, and on with their lives...
But THEY'RE ALWAYS ATTACHED TO YOU...!

Written by Margaret Bergeron
May 2004

GRAMMA'S AND GRAMPA'S...

Count down to the "big" day...
Will it be on time...?
All the phone calls asking...
No sign, no peace of mind...
Then, the middle of night...
"The" phone call does arrive...
Can't seem to get our wits in gear...
Let alone, trying to drive...

See your children overwhelmed...
With JOY and FEAR and STRAIN...
"Please, Lord, help them through it..."
"And help 'Mommy' with her pain..."
Watching as a miracle...
Comes into this new day...
Giving new life to all of us...
With loud cries, he seemed to say...

"Thank you, GRAMMA'S and GRAMPA'S..."
"For MAKING my Mom and my Dad..."
"With your love, and God's own hand..."
"It's the best day I've ever had..."
"Today is my own Birthday......."
"So glad you could all be here..."
"All your love was "FELT" by me..."
"Nine months of the past year..."

"I'll try to make you proud of me..."
"There's so much I need to know..."
"God gave me the best parents..."
"And Grandparents that love me so..."
He's our "newest" little bundle...
Our smiles will surely show...
There is no thrill like Grandkids. AND...
Watching your "Children", grow...

Written by Margaret Bergeron
February 25, 1999

DIDN'T FEEL...

Didn't feel like writing...
When I awoke today...
Clouds looked really gloomy...
I had no words to say...

Then I thought of people...
Who cannot SEE the sky...
The ones who'd give a million...
To HEAR a baby cry....

Has never TOUCHED a loved ones face...
Or WALKED all on their own...
TOLD you when they're lonely...
Because they have no HOME...

I didn't feel like writing...
When I awoke today...
The day "looked" truly gloomy...
So I began to pray...

Not just for friends and family...
Like I usually do......
But all that cannot speak or see...
Or hear or walk, like you...

That you would have a perfect day...
One that you can feel...
Not on the outside that you see...
In your heart, where it is real...

Written by Margaret Bergeron
October 1998

YOU MEAN EVERYTHING TO ME…

I've written many poems about…How much I love you so…
"You mean everything to me…" And I want you to know…
Special times and memories… Glances, smiles and tears…
All the different ups and downs…Got us through the years…

Of course, our daughter and our son…Have bonded us for life…
Our vows to honor and respect…When we became husband and wife…
Now, we're getting older… We're grandparents now…
All our wonderful grandkids…Bond us more, somehow…

We've conquered many obstacles… Had enormous amounts of fun…
Adored each other all these years… You are my "Number 1"…
There's nothing that I would not do…When you hurt, I hurt too….
You start a sentence, I finish it… That's how tuned I am to you…

I have a thought, you think it…We laugh, cause we both know…
Our lives are one, forevermore… Wherever we may go…
We have many years to spend… If we are blessed with time…
Holding my hands, kissing my neck… That is so sublime;..

We've been half-way around the world… Moved to at least a dozen places…
Had about twenty dogs and cats…We've had cramped and open spaces…
Suffered hurts and surgeries… Our share of aches and pains…
But, we've had our share of healing… Cause we get well again…

Of course, we've had our bad. times…Mixed in with all the good…
God sure helped us get through those… Somehow, we KNEW He would…
Another part of you I adore…Is, how you love Mom and Dad…
You seem to know, that they are two… Of the dearest blessings we've had…

So, my Darling Billy… I guess you know today…
That you are my heart's delight… In every possible way…!!
One more thing, I can't forget… Every day, my prayer for you…
That God will hold you in His hand.. .Protecting you all day through…

I LOVE YOU, FOREVER… Margaret XOXOXO…2000

A RHYME ALL THE TIME...

If I use a simple word...To help me with a rhyme...
It will make the message move...At just the perfect time...
I read a word upon a page...My mind just makes it gel..
If I read a word like "cow"...This line must read "cow bell'...

If I see another word...Like mice or rice or nice...
The next line simply has to be...Price, advice or spice...
Don't know why it happens...Can't even give you hints...
My mind rhymes words inside my head...Been "rhyming" ever since...

A little inspiration...Sometimes one word will do
Then my thoughts move quickly...'Til I send them off to you...
Sometimes in one afternoon...If I say macaroon...
Whip the egg whites add coconut...And they'll be ready soon...

Or if I need to read a book...I'd check the shelf to take a look...
What recipe that I will cook...Until I found the one I took...
Sometimes, I make rhyming words...When people speak to me...
If the last word they said was "tree"...In my head I would say, "see"...

Or if they said a sentence...Like, "Let's go out to lunch"...
In my head, I may just say..."I'd rather go to brunch"...
So if you see me sometime...Take note of what you say.
I may just keep on rhyming...In my head, the same old way...

And if we should go shopping...And you wanted some new shoes...
I would automatically think...Perhaps you have the blues...
And if you want to exercise...Maybe take a walk...
Words would form inside my head...Like, block or sock or talk...

Is this called a sickness...Or obsession all the time...
I don't know, I'm busy now...Making another rhyme...

I really cannot help it...Sometimes its really fun...
I've even laughed out loud before...When my mind goes on a run...
Like now, my thoughts are faster...Than my pen can even write...
Time to stop, relax a while... Adios, Adieu, Goodnight...

Written by Margaret Bergeron
August 1999

THEY STARTED OUT SO INNOCENT...

They started out so innocent...Many years ago...
Clinging to your pant leg...Thinking they'd never let go...

Went through the same cute stages...Crawling laughing and tears...
Struggling to say those first sweet words...
Learning manners, to get through the years...

School days just like any other...Perhaps a scrape or two...
They learned their social skills and words...
Making friends, like me and you...

Everything looked ordinary...Then one day they lied...
Ended a life of innocence...In return for another that died...

What makes a young child "fall apart"...?
Makes all their "good sense" bad...?
When will all the cries of help...Be heard by a mom or a dad...?

And if a friend or teacher...Suspects a sad or problem child...
It's better to "tell" and be "real wrong"...Than to let that child go wild...

Remember parents and teachers... Pray for guidance, (not wrath)...
For all your children and students...And for ALL that cross their path...

You can't protect them everywhere...No matter how hard you try...
Give them TIME, ATTENTION AND LOVE...
Instead of things you can buy...

There is no value on innocence...The children depend on you...
Give them all the love you can give...It's all you can hope to do...

Written by Margaret Bergeron
May 1998

95

THINK ABOUT...

Waves on the beach...not sand in your swimsuit...

Warm summer nights...not being too hot to sleep...

Picnics at the park...not ants and bees at your table...

Summer vacations...not unpacking when you return home...

Family reunions...not your company staying too long...

Amusement parks and attractions... not the long lines...

Sunny long days, not sunburned skin and wrinkles...

School being out...not dreading school to start...

Celebrating a birthday...not the age you will be...

Spending time with your children....not what to do with them.

Think about...

Today...not tomorrow...
Think about...

Your many blessings...

You won't have time to think about anything else!!!

Written by Margaret Bergeron
July 1997

THE FACE OF A CHILD...

The face of your children...Goes down deeper than looks...
The look in their eyes...Isn't captured in books...

The curve of their mouth...Or the pout of their lips...
Their eyes filled with tears...Or their hands on their hips...

The smile that appears...For no reason at all...
The hugs and the kisses...Well, that says it all...

When they are young...No one loves you like they...
They cling on to your heart...You are their night and day...

When they are grown up...And out of your reach...
Suggestions are made...That, to them, is a "preach"...

You try to respect...Their wishes and such...
But the "parent" comes out...And your idea is not much...

Then the face of your child...Looks at you with disdain...
Their mouth spouts harsh words...Just your crushed heart remain...

Where did your child go...?Are you really so blind...?
They think you were selfish...You think you were kind...

All the years of your giving...(And their taking it too)...
Is thrown up in your face...And the cause blamed on you...

You tried your best, however...Your best is not enough...
You're punished with their silence...And that punishment is tough...

Written by Margaret Bergeron...
March 1998

97

GO TO WHERE GOD PLANTS YOU...

Go to where God plants you...
Then you feel you will belong...

If He uproots you again...
Just sing a mover's song...

He may just put you in a spot...
You do not fit at all...

Never knowing any one...
Like looking at a wall...

You see, you never know just where...
Your influence may touch...

The life, of yet another soul...
Could depend on you so much....

So question not direction...
Don't think of it as gloom...

Go to where God plants you...
Wait for Him to make you bloom...

Written by Margaret Bergeron
June 1998

ONCE IN A WHILE...

Once in a while you meet someone...
That believes in what you do...
Makes your heart feel "all tucked in"...
Accepting "you" for "YOU"....

Months or years can pass right by...
It doesn't matter much...
The next time that you see them...
Your heart "feels" a gentle touch...

Don't like to use the old cliché...
Like a favorite pair of shoes...
So, like a "cozy blanket"....
That covers you and soothes...

"IF" you have a loved one...
That takes your "cares" to heart...
Give them loving gentleness...
That is a place to start...

If you can find just "one" someone...
To make you feel like this...
Surely, you will feel so blessed...
It's a treasure, not to miss...

Written by Margaret Bergeron
August 1998

SOME THINGS NEVER CHANGE...

Like the way a hot bath feels when you are cold...
The way an open freezer feels when you're hot...
The Santa Ana breezes at sundown...
The calm after a storm...
The smell of chocolate chip cookies baking...
The aroma of coffee brewing...
Burnt popcorn...
The light of a match...
Cold sheets...
The warmth from a hot water bottle...
Diving into a cold pool...
A baby's first cry...
A sandy swimsuit...
When you change from a child into an adult...
The nervousness of your first date...
A double rainbow...
Taking off in an airplane...
Landing in an airplane...
Your first love...
Your first car...
Your first kiss...
Breaking up...
Getting lost...
Being found...
Your first checking account...
Your first savings account...
Your first real challenge...
Your first crisis...
Your first solution...
SOME THINGS JUST NEVER CHANGE...

Written by Margaret Bergeron
March 1998

HAVING CHILDREN...

Making the decision to have children...

Is the one job that you can't get fired from...

And you get no pay for it...

You work the longest hours at...

And the responsibility never ends...

Until your children start worrying about you...

And only then, is the circle complete...

What a circle, huh?

Written by Margaret Bergeron
June 1996

HOW CHILDREN LEARN...

It isn't any big surprise...How children learn to speak...
They imitate their parents' words...However strong or weak...

They listen to you on the phone...And from the other room...
They say their little ears might hear...While they are in the womb...

You know they do respond to voice...Like anger, calm and fear...
And all of their reactions...Are learned before one year...

So, if they hear their mom or daddy...Shout, hit, swear or cry...
They will think it's acceptable...And you will then know why...

Where else can your little ones...Pick up their ways to act...
Too young to learn from anyone else...
You taught them...as a matter of fact...

Later, they learn from teachers...With actions and words from their peers...
Trying them out on their families...Or anyone else that can hear...

Then one day the little mouth, (that you thought was clean)...
Spouts words... (that hang on like a rope)...
You look so surprised... (with your little tyke)..
As you wash out their mouth with some soap...

Then you say to them..."Where'd you learn such a word..?"
"And don't you say that anymore...!"
Your little child says, "I learned it from you"...
"When you yelled at the man in the store"...

You'll soon be seeing yourself in your child...
And you may just not like what you see...
So start out today and fill up their hearts...
With the thing you would like them to be...

Written by Margaret Bergeron
February 1998

102

GOSSIP...

It's better not to have a mouth...
Than to say an unkind word...
No matter if you whisper...
Gossiping will be heard...

The damage from a wagging tongue...
Speaking loosely, so untrue...
Can follow someone all of their life...
Hope and pray, it is not you...

Gossip starts from one loose tale...
Told about another...
Then grows to such proportions...
'Til it destroys the other...

Venom from a snake bite...
Hurts less than a word untrue...
Especially when you hear the words...
Were spoken about you...

Can gossips take the words all back...?
Sure, but when they do...
They won't be telling anyone...
That they took them back from you...

Written by Margaret Bergeron
October 1997

BY CHANCE

By chance we got to live near you ?

By chance, I don't think so...

Cause in God's plan, He knew just how...

Our great friendship would grow...

Not cause we borrow sugar...

Or share a drink or two...

Just cause you listen when we talk...

You don't judge the things we do…

And we just want to say "Thank you"...

Written by Margaret Bergeron
September 1997

COURAGE...

It takes a lot of courage...
To leave your comfort zone...
Maybe you think of going away...
Or buying a brand new home...

Maybe you've already ventured out...
And left all you had behind...
Leaving friends, old jobs for new...
Seeking and hoping to find...

It takes courage and lots of trust...
To start your life anew...
Depending only on yourself...
Just God, yourself and you...

There may be disappointments...
I guarantee a few...
But you will feel accomplishment...
In the little things you do...

Courage in starting over...
Is worth the hurdles you jump...
The further you go towards your goal...
Takes you farther over the hump...

Written by Margaret Bergeron
October 1997

WHAT IF...

What if...

The mail didn't come...The lights didn't work...
The grocery store...Had no cashier clerk...

The milk was all lumpy...Our food all had mold...
Because all of our refrigerators...Would not get cold...

The banks had no money...And we didn't have bills...
Our checks wouldn't bounce...And we wouldn't need wills..

We didn't have curfew...And we had no more crime...
We could still stroll the beach...With no fear anytime...

We had no disease...And a "cure" for the cold...
We all lived and loved...Until we all got real old...
What if...
Everyone had...A nice thing to say...You got hugged
in the morning...And kissed, everyday...
Everyone...everywhere...Looked just the same...
Nowhere could anyone...Place any blame...

No one to hate and no one to fear...(And instead of dodging a gun...)
We all tried to think of "good" things to do...
And all of our days were "just fun"...

A stroll in the park, could once more...Seem relaxing and calming and be...
A place for a picnic with family and friends...
While letting our children run free...

Our schools and our teachers...Could have just what they need...
Learning would be fun again...And our children could succeed...

What if...

We couldn't imagine...Or couldn't think...?

Written by Margaret Bergeron
October 1997

106

IN THE MIDDLE OF THE NIGHT...

When everyone else is sleeping...And dreams roll around your brain...
Possums scavenge, raccoons search..."Trash" is their terrain...

But also in the still of night....Unaware, since you don't see...
Are the loving hands of the people...That take care of you and me...

Firefighters are hard at work...And paramedics too...
Saving lives throughout the night...Is a loving job they do...

Hospitals and doctors...Hardly get to sleep...
Nurses helping with the sick...And caring for moms as they weep...

Attendants turning patients...Smoothing out their woes...
Caring for your loved ones...While you're sleeping, heaven knows...

Bakers baking your favorite breads...Very late at night...
Bagels, donuts, fresh croissants...So that they taste just right...

Emergency men and highway crews...Patching up the street...
Snowplows cleaning up the roads...Trash men keeping paths neat...

Always on the phone lines...Are great folks working there...
Helping you with emergencies...No matter when or where...

And don't forget the moms and dads...Pacing the floors at night...
Looking as the clock ticks by...Hoping their family is all right...

There are a certain number of you...That cannot sleep too good...
You carry the burdens of everyone...Who lay
sleeping ... (like you should)...

Written by Margaret Bergeron...
February 1998

IT'S NEVER TOO LATE FOR YOU...

When life demands too much from you...
When you cannot keep the pace...
Things are falling down on you...Clouding up your space...

Time is not sufficient...For all that you must do...
No time to even sleep enough...Just eating fast food too...

You're always pushing harder...Trying hard to please...
Haven't had a moments rest...Or noticed the cool breeze...

Everywhere you go is rushed...No minutes for you to stop...
You watch your list get longer..."Family" no longer on top...

What is it you are striving for...?Is money at the end...?
Will you only buy more "stuff"...?With no time for you to spend...?

One day you'll get up tired...Your vim and vigor bruised...
You'll have nice things surrounding you...
That your friends and family used...

All your work and hours...For this "grand life" you cast...
You're forgetting to "LIVE" it...Now, some of it has passed...

You look around your quiet house...Everyone is grown...
Your family is so busy now...They're all just "on their own"...

You were always "GOING TO" take...Time off and have some fun...
Show your loving family, that...Life had just begun...

Put God at the beginning ...Of everything you do...
He will help make sense of it...He'll put you in order too...

Should you have planned it sooner...?Wish you could start anew?
This day is just beginning...IT'S NEVER TOO LATE FOR YOU...!

Written by Margaret Bergeron...1997

FEELING ON THE INSIDE
(or) INSIDE OF HERE

I'm on the inside looking…
Out onto this big life…
I want to say that from in here…
I'm the same vivacious wife…
The years have passed and with it time…
Moved quickly and fine with you…
Yet, age has probably left its mark…
But inside, I'm still twenty-two…

I don't quite feel the gravity…
Inside this shell of mine…
I don't feel that I have changed…
In here, I feel just fine…
Aside from all the aches and pains…
Caused from the passing of time…
And getting tired earlier…
From in here, I am sublime…

I look at you through loving eyes…
A thoughtful man I see…
Looking inside me…to my heart…
You always take good care of me…
A lot of blemishes we have…
On these bodies we are given…
But God made them disposable…
So He could take us…to heaven…

So what I'm really saying is…
Thank-you for being kind…
For all the loving words and care…
And to "my" faults…acting blind…
Thank you for teaching me so much…
And treating me tenderly…
Cause from in here, my lifelong love…
You're the only man I see…

Written by Margaret Bergeron …
May 1997

A FRIEND...

If any of you have a friend...
That is there no matter what...
If they will drop their task at hand...
To help you in a spot...

If you can really, truly say...
Your friend will help you smile...
And stop at nothing till they do...
Then go the extra mile...

And when you really need this friend...
When you think they can't do more...
There they are so willing...
Standing at your door...

Where do they get their tender hearts..?
They never do complain...
Knowing that their only pay...
Is just to ease your pain...

What do you do for friends like this...?
How do you help them too...?
You listen and return their love...
SOMEDAY, THEY MAY NEED YOU...!

Written by Margaret Bergeron...1998

TEARS...or WHY WE CRY...

All the cares and worries...Stack up in your dear head...
Pushing all the tension, 'til...Your eyes start turning red...
Pressure builds behind your eyes...As if to break your heart...
Pours out of those tear ducts...From every liquid part...

Sometimes for no good reason...But, who's to say what's good...?
Tear ducts are just what they are...If you want to cry...you should...
Holding back emotion...Cannot be understood...
It just upsets your stomach...And that is not so good...

If men and boys would cry like us...It could ease their troubled minds...
Emotion flowing down the drain...Could make our world, more kind...
It takes a bit of pressure...To make our tear ducts "puff"...
The water that flows down our cheeks...Just cleans our eyes enough.........

It lets us see what's causing...The tears that freely flow...
Crying is an emotion...In case you didn't know...
It can come from sadness...Or happiness, extreme...
Even come from fright or shock...When you wake up from a dream...

Next time that your eyes sting....Don't blink away those tears...
Release all that emotion...And your tears will disappear...

Written, by Margaret Bergeron
November 1999

RULES ARE MADE...

Rules are made for you to keep...
Not overlooked or broken...
Otherwise, our world would be...
Not worth a wooden token...

Its bad enough, that so many...
Don't care about the law...
They make it hard on everyone...
And rub your patience raw...

Every night the news is bleak...
One crime follows another...
People hurting children...
And turning against their brother...

Breaking a rule or law today...
Means tomorrow will be less...
For you and your family to enjoy...
The future will be a mess...!

Rules are not "made to be broken"...
And are not hard to obey...
Besides they are for you and me...
So just try it out today...

Written by Margaret Bergeron
April 1998

PICTURE YOURSELF...

Picture yourself on a hilltop...
With snow and ice on the ground...
Doesn't it cool you and give you a feel...
Of winter and calm all around...

Now sit on a patch of grass at the park...
With the sun streaming down through the trees...
Picture yourself with no cares in the world...
Then relax and enjoy the cool breeze...

Stroll on the beach and pick out a spot...
To leisurely lay on the sand...
Watch how the waves continually form...
And the foam and the water meet land...

Picture yourself in the place you like best...
And be there each day for a bit...
Enjoy every minute of visiting there...
Letting go of your cares while you sit...

Because you'll never get rid of your problems...
Each day a new one appears...
But letting yourself have a moment of calm...
Will help you maintain through the years...

Written by Margaret Bergeron
October 1997

FIRST DAY JITTERS...

Whether you're starting a brand new job...
Or the scary, first day of class...
We all know that your stomachs churn...
Fearing this feeling won't pass...

The moment that you wake up...
(If you even slept at all)...
The panic will begin to start...
When your knees tell you to fall...

Breakfast is out of the question...
You can barely rinse your mouth...
Toothpaste, this morning, makes you gag...
Your insides are going south...

You put your brand new clothes on...
And try so hard to grin...
You've waited so long, for this big day...
And it is about to begin...

Will they like me, will I succeed...?
The questions and worries abound...
All the way to school or work...
Doubts seem to merry-go-round...

So...the final moment comes...
You are standing at the door...
Walking in, you realize...
You are frozen to the floor...

Someone smiles, you loosen up...
You think, "It's not so bad"...
Those First Day Jitters are going away...
And you are feeling glad...

Written by Margaret Bergeron
September 1997

CHOICES...

Dry toast or fluffy pancakes...?
Crisp hash browns or fruit...?
Real fresh eggs or fake ones...?
Should you give bacon the boot...?

Sweetener or pure sugar...?
Butter or non-stick spray..?
Whole milk or the non-fat kind..?
Choices make up every day...

Eat raw or cooked veggies...?
Baked potatoes or fried...?
Salad with no good dressing...?
Or set off to the side...?

Juicy, crispy chicken...?
Or baked with no visible skin...?
Biscuits with lots of gravy...?
Or unsalted crackers, so thin...?

Eat ice cream with toppings...?
Or, no ice cream at all...?
Non-fat chocolate brownies...?
Or a plain dry popcorn ball...?

Vitamins and health juice...?
Oat bran, fiber and rice...?
Makes us all feel 'perky"...
Though the taste is not so nice...

Keep on eating healthy...
Stretch and exercise each day...
Eat dessert " before" you do...!!!!
And you will be okay...!

Written by Margaret Bergeron
January 1999

NO MOOD...

Kinda blah...
Kinda yuk...
Kinda nothing...
Kinda stuck...
Kinda sad...
Kinda poopy...
Kinda bored...
Kinda droopy...
Kinda restless...
Kinda tired...
Kinda nervous...
Kinda wired...
Kinda edgy...
Kinda jumpy...
Kinda twitchy...
Kinda grumpy...
Kinda tense...
Kinda weary...
Kinda sleepy...
Kinda teary...
Kinda worn out...
Kinda drained...
Kinda labored...
Kinda strained...
Melancholy...
Kinda dull...
Kinda dismal...
That is all...
Glad this day...
Will not last...
Soon enough...
It will...Be past....

Written by Margaret Bergeron...2005

DO YOUR VERY BEST...

No one can be perfect...
We're different from the rest...
Some are smarter, some are not...
We can only do our best...
Some rely on beauty...
Or talent in their voice...
Some have minds for science...
Others, paint, by choice...
Some are good with people...
Helping in their care...
Some are great with fabric...
Designing what we wear...
We all have a favorite thing...
That puts us to the test...
Whatever your special quality...
Be sure to do your best...

Do your hands do all the work...?
Or does your mind exceed.?
Do you own a business...?
Or pull somebody's weeds...?
Do you help the public...?
Keeping peace upon our streets...?
Do you buy our real estate...?
Or sell us fish and meat...?

Do you know how many jobs...?
There are, that you all do...?
Everyone, DOING THEIR BEST...
Will make it good for you...
If you manage people's jobs...
Remember, that _you_ too...
Will help create the very best...
If _Your best_ is what you do...
No matter what you do today...
Whether working or at rest...
Have fun while you're doing it...
And GIVE IT YOUR VERY BEST...!

Written. by Margaret Bergeron...March 17. 2000

CLOUDS...

Always different...
Never the same...
No single cloud...
Even gets its own name...

Some are of rain...
Others of snow...
Some look like angels...
They float to and fro...

Some are so thick...
You'd think you could stand...
On a piece of the fluff...
Or grab hold with your hand...

Some look like people...
Your eyes see a face...
A cat or a dog...
Or some special place...

Before your own eyes...
It stretches away...
Every one is so perfect, but...
Not a one ever stays...

Written By Margaret Bergeron
July 2001

BUTTERMILK SKY...

Looking up at fluffy clouds...
Scattered about as they fly...
Mixed with the blue and yellowy sun...
Our own special "Buttermilk Sky"...

Kind of curdled, smooth, with lumps...
Just you, my love, and I...
Holding hands as we pray for peace...
To God, in the "Buttermilk sky...

It may not sound too romantic...
Except to you and me...
We know just what it looks like...
It's quite a sight to see...

Let others call the clouds by name...
We will not ask them why...
We will just sit still and gaze...
At our "Beautiful Buttermilk Sky"...

Written by Margaret
March 2006

WHY THINGS HAPPEN WHEN THEY DO...

How are we supposed to know...Why things happen when they do...?
How the day or night unfolds...Can ruin good intentions too...

Take a stroll or ride your board...Going your own pace...
Stop to cheer a lonely chap...Seemed to need a friendly face...

You made a peddler happy...By lending him your ear...
Then he really caused you grief...By letting minors near...

You tried to keep those "little kids"...From getting into trouble...
Only to find out later... That they sure crossed you...double...!

There is an "age old" saying...That "nice guys finish last"...
But, it sure depends on when...You think the time has passed...

It must have been a heartache...For everyone involved...
Seeing you inside that place...Because, you're "oh, so loved"...

It seems you made the best of it...(You probably made some friends)...
I'm sure you made some bad guys think...Where their life could surely end...

So, again we see that God...STILL has the "upper hand."...
Prayers and faith and family...Still rule across this land...!

So thank Our Lord for miracles...And for the family you were given...
Pray for those who do not know...The reason they are living...

Keep your smile and, friendly ways..."Things just happen when they do"...
To let us know that God's in charge...And, His love is always true...

Written by Margaret Bergeron
01-03-2000

COMFORT ZONE...

Why is it we get so nervous...? Or anxious, scared, afraid...?
Of moving out of our comfort zone...Even after the plans are made...?
We've paid our money, taken off work...
Packed our bags and said good-bye...
Kissed our husbands and our kids...And we're off, but with a sigh...!

The cats and dogs attended to...Food and treats, there's plenty...
Why are we so hesitant...We'll make friends, (and there are many)...!
You've stepped out of your comfort zone...A scary place to be...
But God will fill that scary place...He'll hold on to you and me...

So you sign in and get your key...You open up the door...
To all new faces, and once again...You're scared a little more...
You pick your roommate and your bed...You wonder, "Does it show"...?
How self-conscious that you are...Does anybody know...?

The week-end finally does begin...You're blessed beyond belief...
The message God had planned for you...Has given you relief...
The music, singing, laughter...The tears fall just like rain...
God has brought you to this place...To make you whole again...

Come to Him, <u>just as we are</u>...Leave all the fluff behind...
He will give you all you need...He is honest, true and kind...
He loves us with our "Shabby" clothes...Or with "Designer" jeans...
He loves us with our flaws and woes...
"Menopause", "Old Age", or "Teens"...

He sees our hearts, down to our souls...And loves us, every one...
In fact, He loves us all <u>SO</u> much...That He <u>Sacrificed His Son...</u>
We've made new friends and shared our lives...How could we be afraid...?
We all are chosen women...Whose sins have all been paid...!

So when you feel afraid about...Stepping from your comfort zone...
Many others felt the same...Before they left their home...
Now our time is about to close...What a blessing this has been...
Every life has changed and now...God will send us home again...
"Thank you", all our new friends...And <u>EVERYONE</u> that took a part...
By taking that step from your comfort zone...
And for opening up your heart...

Written By Margaret Bergeron...May 4, 2002   From Shabby to Chic Retreat

THINK WHAT WE WOULD MISS...

If you didn't turn the corner…
Just think what you could miss…
Seeing Our Lord in a garden…
On a morning just like this…

Get up and pray for someone…
Don't let the moment go…
Pray for those around you…
Or, for those you do not know…

There will still be troubles…
That you will have to bear…
But God will never leave you…
He will still be there…

Equip yourself with blessings…
No matter what they are…
God has given <u>you</u> a gift…
You can be a shining star…

God will surely stir your nest…
Your resting place, your bed…
Giving you the wings to fly…
And "His Shoulder" to rest your head…

He will never let you fall…
His arms will hold you close…
"Be still and <u>know</u> that "HE" is God…
When your heart needs Him the most…

Whatever stirs in you right now…
Give it to God today…
You'll be surprised how He will take…
Your worries and cares away…

Written by Margaret Bergeron…2006

A GOOD PERSON...

Someone who first thinks about...
The needs and cares of you...
Sees to all the details...
Before the day is through...

Never seems to mind too much...
When things don't work out right...
Keeps their wits about them...
Most every day and night...

Makes you feel important...
Listens with deep care...
Truly tries to help you out...
Is always, always there...

Has a calming quality...
Every time they're near...
Friendship is all they want from you...
And sometimes to lend an ear...

Always there in bad times...
And for the good times too...
Showing up with love and words...
Always a friend to you...

If you have a friend like this...
A good person, honest and true...
God has blessed you richly...
By giving this friend to you...

Some have friends that come and go...
Some no friends at all...
Do you want to renew a friendship...?
Just...pick up the phone and call...

Written by Margaret Bergeron...March 2003

I JUST WANT TO MATTER...

I just want to matter in this world...
To leave a "Matter Mark"...
Do something you'll remember...
Before I disembark...

If I could make others happy...
Or change a life or two...
Give some, "Unconditional" love...
And matter to all of you...

If my words could make a difference...
Make you think of something good...
Take comfort in my rhyming...
Like I'm hoping that you would...

If I could just open up my heart...
And let you see inside...
You'd see how much you "Matter" to me...
There is nothing I could hide...

So when you hear me say the words...
"I just want to Matter to you"...
It means my life is so fulfilled...
Because, "YOU MATTER TO ME TOO"...

Written by Margaret Bergeron
March 2006

THE CLOCK KEEPS GOING FORWARD...

Time passes by so quickly...
Each hour, without a sound...
The little hand steadily does its job...
The big hand...follows it around...
It can't go back, just forward...
It only goes one way...
So after one of them passes...
You start another day...
Pretty soon, a week goes by...
A month, a year or more...
Where did all that time go...?
Closed up, behind, no more...
What happened to the time, you say...?
How could it go so fast...?
"Time is the thing that happens..."
"To make yesterday your past..."
What did you do with yesterday...?
Did it go out in style...?
Did you make a difference ...?
Did you make "another" smile...?
Did you take the time to ponder...?
Over what is best to do...?
Did you forget to pray about...?
What God would have for you...?
While you are looking at the clock...
(A hundred times a day...)
Whether at work or playing...
There are things you need to say...
You'll NEVER get those hours back...
That time has slipped away...
You WILL BE MISSING SOMETHING GREAT...
IF YOU FORGET TO PRAY...

Written By Margaret Bergeron
September 22, 2001

JUST LIKE BUBBLES...

Bubbles are pretty, funny things...They reflect everything, all around...
Life could be like those bubbles...Floating, until stopped on the ground...

Do you wonder, "How much is enough?"...
Why is it we always want more...?
Comparing ourselves to the Jones'...What do we do that for...?

Who are the Jones' anyway?... Do you know who they are...?
Are they gatherers of stuff?... Do they have a better car...?

Did someone tell them, "They are IT?"...The ones we set out to beat...?
Or is it just a scam for all...The people that we meet...?

Are THESE Jones' happier?...Or do they just want more...?
Because they can't be satisfied...With what they had before...?

How do we really view them?...Are they just the ones to pass...?
Get more & more & more in debt...How long will this stuff last...?

It is better to be satisfied...With what you have right now...
Than always wanting something else...Or, when can we get it, or, how...

Clothes, cars, houses, jewelry...We all possess a few...
Just don't make them Number One...You can't take them with you...

When was the last time that you saw...
A hearse with a U Haul for storage...?
It may sound silly at the thought...But Heaven won't pay your mortgage...

Treasures on earth do not last long...Where moth and rust destroy...
Also thieves break in and steal...Your riches and your toys...

Set your heart on things above...It will surely relieve the pressure...
Keep values, friends and family...And Heaven as your treasure...

Written by Margaret Bergeron
June 2001

SPLISH SPLASH...

We have a special Splash Group...We meet most every day...
In our lovely, pool and spa...Weather...come what may...!

The water is so perfect...The sky and palms above...
Makes us glad to be alive...And bonds us all with love...

We never let a day go by...Without some love to share...
We ALL have our problems...Sometimes, we say a prayer...

Dancing to the music...Singing if we want...
With closed eyes or thinking...Floating, as we find our spot...

Makes us smile and be so glad...Sometimes someone will cry...
Sharing each others burdens...Without even asking why...

Never let a chance go by...Without some love to give...
It helps all those around you...Love pours out like a sieve...

Our Splash Group gives us confidence...While helping us relax...
Working out the aches and pains...And strengthening our backs...

We all have issues in our days...That helps, <u>so</u>, when we share...
There's none like our pool friendships...We truly know we care...

And when we see the clouds float by...A rainbow, or drop of rain...
It reminds us just how blessed we are...And we start all over again...

Written by Margaret Bergeron...2002

IT AMAZES ME…

It amazes me to see the sun…Coming up, the same each day…
It amazes me how it makes its path…And we don't miss a single ray…
It amazes me how the days it rains…Somewhere else, the sun is bright…
And somewhere else, when we have day…Then, they are having night…
It amazes me that people look up…And see such different sights…
Some can witness miracles…Others, just day or night…
It amazes me how the moon just hangs…And waits to light the sky…
Waiting patiently for the sun to set…Without even asking, why…
Sometimes when we are extra blessed…We can see the moon and sun…
Hanging out together…Giving us a little fun…
And then there is the rain and snow…That amazes me to the core…
Knowing exactly when to fall…Or when to freeze some more…
It amazes me that the wind that blows…Can clear our air and hills…
It amazes me that someone would try…To burn it all, at will…
It amazes me that a single rose…Doesn't prove to all that see…
That God has made this earth for us…And the best is yet to be…
It amazes me as I'm sitting here…Everything just seems so clear…
This is just our waiting place…This is where we shed our tears…
So, tomorrow, when the sun comes up…To greet another day…
Be amazed at how it warms your face…And you'll know just what to say…
It amazes me how the birds can fly…And they squawk and sing and sway…
Building nests and talking…Just like any other day…
It amazes me that they never worry…Or fret about a thing…
Except to protect a little one…Or some danger the nest could bring…
It amazes me that the bees and flies…And spiders and bugs and ants…
Can go on living together…And it amazes me, <u>we can't</u>…
It amazes me in this huge world…So spacious, wide and far…
That people want to make it theirs…So creating a constant war…
It amazes me every time I think…That there's just one thing to do…
One Perfect Savior died for our sins…
We need to follow His instructions too…
It amazes me how simple it is…When I close my eyes to pray…
How God already knows His plan… For every single day…
So worry doesn't change the tide…Wonderings' still a fret…
Nothing we do, on this side…Has ever changed things yet…
So be amazed in all things…Keep your heart upon the Prize…
<u>"BE STILL AND KNOW THAT HE IS GOD"</u>…
<u>And HE'S right before your eyes…</u>

Written by Margaret Bergeron
October 2007

MONEY...

Money can't mend a broken heart...Money can't give you time...
It cannot make the wrong things right...Or make your family fine...

It cannot buy you happiness...Or show your kids you care...
Can't buy more time with those you love...Or let them know you're there...

You can't take money with you...What matters, you will find...
You can't rewind a wasted life...You must leave it all behind..

The people, the experiences...That's the lesson learned from this...
Money only pays the bills...Does not buy eternal bliss...

Give me friends and family...Give me days to laugh and play...
Hugs and kisses from my kids...Knowing that I'm loved all day...

Things that can't be taken away...Like warmth and smiles and heart...
Feelings that light up my way...Right, from the very start...

So give me love, not money...Though, it may pay the bills...
It doesn't last and only hurts...Relationships, it kills...

Things are nice, don't get me wrong...But, how long can they last...?
A nice few things, a fancy life...Then, all of a sudden, it's past...

Pick a rose and you will find...More happiness and joy...
God made every leaf and petal...Not like a store bought toy...

It's funny how we think that all...the money we get or spend...
Belongs to us, instead of GOD...It's ALL HIS, in the end...

Money can't buy happiness...It can't mend a broken heart...
Love's the only thing that lasts...God made every single part...

Written by Margaret Bergeron
January 2008

T.V. TUBE AND TELEVISION...

It was such a great invention...
How could you ever guess...?
That "square box" could do so much...
While making you do less...!
You can spot a T. V. buff...
Just look outside and see...
Weeds are growing wildly...
No time to trim that tree...
And they made T. V. dinners...
Just for T. V. trays...
And T.V. guides, so you won't miss...
A program while you graze...!
And then they made "REMOTE CONTROL"...
How could they be so mean...?
Each day the battle to be "BOSS"...
Scanning channels on your screen...!
Ever watched a complete show...?
While watching with your mate...?
Frustration, (maybe arguments)...
A real live "T.V. Gate"...
Of course, you can watch videos...
Computers, weather too...
Discovery, Learning, Cooking...
Just to name a few...
The children watch cartoons and such...
And Rescue Nine- One -One...
Wheel of Fortune and Jeopardy...
Can make your viewing fun...
Don't look at T.V. as the enemy...
Although it can make you "stressed"...
When your family's watching it...
Instead of getting dressed...
So, before you call it a problem...
And "Tube" is all you see...
Think of all the good it brings...
What would you do "Without T.V."...?

Written by Margaret Bergeron
February 1998

FORGIVE...

No matter what you've done to others...
Or what they've done to you...
HE expects us to forgive...
He forgave His enemies too...
He died to save our souls from hell...
In every circumstance...
Before we even came to sin...
He forgave us "in advance"...
Sometimes it's really hard to forgive...
When you feel you were betrayed...
Think of how Our Savior felt...
When He lost the friends "HE MADE"...
"I spent many hours of agony"...
"Upon the Cross THAT DAY"...
"SO THAT YOU WOULD FORGIVE EACH OTHER"...
"In a very SIMPLE way"...
"No matter what's been done to you"...
"Whoever hurts your pride"...
"Remember, I already PAID THE PRICE"...
"I GAVE YOU A FREE RIDE"...
"All you have to do for ME"...
"Is, FORGIVE, just as I DO"...
"It's not an easy task, I KNOW"...
"But easier, than what I DID FOR YOU"...
"I'M reminding you "through someone else"...
"Because, I think you fear"...
"That forgiving someone that you love"...
"Could calm that rage you hear"...
"Consider all those around you"...
"Whose hearts are hurting so"...
"LOOK TO ME, RELEASE THE ANGER"...
"HAND IT OVER... LET IT GO"...
"I know you find it hard to believe"...
"That these words are written through me"...
But, GOD woke me up with EVERY WORD...
"That HE wanted you to see"...

Written by GOD, through Margaret Bergeron...
July 2006

REMEMBER ME...

Remember when you go to sleep...
Remember when you wake...
Remember when you say your prayers...
Remember when you bake...

Remember when you pull a weed...
Or plant a pretty flower...
Remember when you wake up late...
Or at a crazy hour...

Remember when you're driving...
Or in a crowded room...
Maybe in the grocery store...
Or shopping for perfume...

Remember when you're lonely...
Or even when you're not...
Remember when you're most confused...
Or when you're cold or hot...

Remember when you need a smile...
A hug, or just a look...
Remember when you need a friend...
That you can't find in a book...

I lived my life so fully...
Felt your love in every way...
Remember me in God's Garden...
Like a flower He holds each day...

And when you think I am not there...
Remember...I am a part...
Of everything in front of you...
And...I'm always in your heart...

Written By Margaret Bergeron ...1997

ANGELS ON PATROL...

There's a reason for everything...
Don't know what it can be...
Some things seem to go so wrong...
As you can surely see...

Things are building up so high...
Out of your control...
Stress, emotion and your fears...
Are taking a great toll...

Waiting in an office...
Not knowing what's to come...
Giving all your fears to God...
Wish you could just go home...

Needles surgeries and pain...
X-Rays, MRI's...
Doctors know just what to do...
We sometimes cry and sigh...!

Want your life back normal...
Wish it could be so...
Waiting for your turn today...
But you really just want to go...!

Our bodies are built perfect...
Then age can creep on in...
Accidents can also cause...
"Conditions" to begin...

Many times you want to say...
"Enough, please don't do more"...
Until you find a quiet place...
Give it to God, once more...

So, if you think you can't go on...
If you feel out of control...
Close your eyes and know that there are....
"Angels on Patrol"...

Written by Margaret Bergeron...2004

TODAY…

TODAY IS NOT YOUR NORMAL DAY…

YOUR OH – SO - WHAT- DOESN'T MATTER DAY…

TODAY IS LIKE THE KIND OF DAY…

THE - WANT - TO - CLICK - YOUR – HEELS – UP - DAY…

THE KISS – ALL – YOUR – PROBLEMS
– AWAY – KIND – OF - DAY…

IT'S THE DAY – TO – DO – YOUR – SMILING – DAY…

BLOW ALL – THE COBWEBS – AWAY –KIND OF DAY…

AND SCREAM – ATOP – A – MOUNTAIN – DAY…

EAT STEAK AND CHOCOLATE AND WHITE BREAD DAY…

BAKED POTATOES, SOUR CREAM AND BUTTER DAY…

WALK ON THE BEACH – WITH – NO – SUNSCREEN – DAY…

DREAM OF HEAVEN AND HAPPINESS DAY…

THE - GLAD – TO – BE – A PART OF – LIFE – KIND OF DAY…

TODAY'S THE DAY TO CELEBRATE THAT YOU WERE BORN…!!!

WE ALL CELEBRATE YOU AND THE LIFE THAT YOU LIVE…

AND THE FINE EXAMPLE THAT YOU GIVE…

TO ALL OF YOUR FAMILY AND FRIENDS…

HAPPY BIRTHDAY FROM ALL OF US…!

Written by Margaret Bergeron…1999

THE ONE AND ONLY JESUS...

He knew at such an early age...This fateful day would be...
When He would give His body up...To die and set us free...
He knew He had to do it...His Father told Him so...
All His days led to this one...And today He had to go...
Apostles, family and friends...Were with Him that last week...
His closest 12 shared one last meal...Then, Judas kissed His cheek...
He went into a garden...To pray that this "might pass"...
He knew they would be coming soon...This night would be His last...
He said, "If you could stay awake"..."Please pray with Me tonight"...
Instead, they left Him all alone...And slept until dawn's light...
So many soldiers took Him...This Loving, Giving, Lord...
If He wanted He could make them, fall...He wouldn't need a sword...
He knew what they must do right then...No other choice could be...
His fate was sealed by just a kiss...To nail Him to a tree...
The One and Only Jesus...Endured the worst of pain...
So we could be in Heaven...Today, He must be slain...
So, on that day so long ago...Though none of us were there...
Even then, He knew us all...And counted every hair...
He knew what we'd be doing...And how we'd live our days...
How long that it would take us...To follow all His ways...
So when you think of how it hurt...Unbearable and so grim...
The pain we feel inside our hearts...Was so much worse for Him...
The One and Only Jesus...Took on the world that day...
He Suffered, Died, and Rose again...He took our sin away...
All He asks of us is this...Love Him with all your heart...
Love your neighbor as yourself...This day is a good day to start...
The One and Only Jesus...Is waiting so patiently...
Never let a day go by...Without thinking of that tree...

Written by Margaret Bergeron...2007

SPECIAL DOCTORS CARE…
DOCTOR CHIKOVANI AND DOCTOR DOBKIN

It's so important to get…Special doctors care…
Take their time and really listen…Like they really have time to spare…

Looks at you and seems to …Care about your life…
All that you are going through…Even if you've got some strife…

Such a special talent…To have, if you're a Doc…
Smiles and cares and knows their stuff…!And even to have a talk…!

Tries to be the best of help…To get through all your ills…
Takes the time to explain what's wrong…And how to take your pills…

Not many can be a Doctor…It takes a special breed…
You must love being around people…For that, there's a special need…!

If your Doctors make you rushed…Or do not seem to care…
CHIKOVANI and DOBKIN will fix you up… Always, always there…

They HAD to take to me real fast…I had problems at the start…
But, then they knew the pain I felt…They truly showed their hearts…

The staff is just the best there is…They greet you at the door…
CHIKOVANI and DOBKIN…Are worth getting up for…

So thank you, MY DEAR DOCTORS…
You've worked magic on my spine…
You're in my prayers every day…I'm feeling better than fine!…

Written and composed by Margaret Bergeron…2007 and 2008
With many, many thanks

SEEDS OF CHANGE...

"Let your roots grow into HIM"...
The Colossians verses say...
"Draw up nourishment from HIM"...
Every single day...

"See that you go on growing"...
"In the Lord and become strong"...
Become "vigorous" as well...
Those words cannot be wrong...

As we encounter, each "Season in Life"...
Passing flowers and sweetness all day...
Tucked in between the beauty, are thorns...
With thistles and weeds, on the way...

God nourishes us to replenish our souls...
Leading us to the paths we should walk...
Even though we may stumble, and at times, lose our step...
He has our hearts in HIS lock...!

The beauty and perfection as you look at the rose...
The aroma, the dew from the rain...
Even though a thorn, on the stem of a rose...
Can stick you and cause you some pain...

And, if along our life's journey...
We forget to pull out the weeds...
Our beautiful garden aroma...
Will return to unplanted seeds...

The seeds that grow in a garden...
Much like the seeds in our souls...
God plants those seeds in both places...
We water them, so they can grow...

Written By Margaret Bergeron
October 2001

LOVE...IS THE GREATEST OF ALL...

No matter how we speak the words...
Of men or angels too...
Love must fully fill each one...
Or the meaning won't come through...

Have you the gift of Prophecy...?
Moving mountains from your faith...?
But do not have the love of God...?
Then you are an empty space...

Love is patient...It does not rush...
Loves kindness comes to call...
Envy does not stand a chance...
When love can cover all...

Love doesn't boast...not rude or proud...
Does not seek itself...
Love's slow to anger, at all times...
No "wrongs" stored upon the shelf...

No delight in "getting even"...
Rejoices in truth and fact...
Always protects and trusts and hopes...
Perseverance kept in tact...

We're taught that Love can never fail...
We trust in God above...
Faith, Hope and Love, the three remain...
But the Greatest of these is LOVE...

Written by Margaret Bergeron
June 2003

OLD WOODEN FENCE...

What would the old wooden fence say...?
If we could only know...
Old prospectors and farmers...
Passed by, many years ago...

It's seen so many winters...
Survived a hundred storms...
At times the snow covered it so...
That's why it looks so worn...

It kept the livestock safely held...
Kept other critters out...
Kept the cows and sheep together...
Not wandering about...

How many folks leaned on that fence...?
And shared a dream or two...?
How many stories has it heard...?
If, we only knew...!

The winds have blown right through it...
The sun has baked it dry.. .
It's leaning, crooked and paint worn off...
But, it's still standing... why...?

If only that old fence could talk...
I wonder what we'd hear...?
So many people passed right by...
For, oh, so many years...

Sitting on that worn out fence...
With hammer and nails in tow...
Trying to make it stay the same...
As it was so long ago...

Written By Margaret Bergeron... July 2001

THE HAND...

Picture the biggest, strongest hand...
With the fingers opened wide...
Put yourself in the "PALM OF GOD"...
Where you have nothing to hide...
Take with you, your doubts and fears...
Bring your troubles and illness and shame...
Carry up your baggage of worry...
Your anger, your hurts and your blame...
Don't forget to bring all your pain...
Your upsets, your headaches and stress...
Please remember to pack ALL YOU'VE HIDDEN...
And what else got you into this mess...
Your bags are all packed as you climb to the top...
You lay down your troubles and strife...
And, as you let go you can't seem to leave...
The THINGS that hurt MOST in your life...
You're holding on as God watches you...
Dragging this "ONE" thing back home...
He looks at you and plucks it away...
"<u>YOU</u> CAN'T DO THAT BIG THING ALONE"...
"JUST LEAVE IT WITH <u>ME</u>, I TOLD YOU <u>I'D</u> HELP"...
"HAND IT OVER, JUST GIVE IT TO <u>ME</u>"...
"HOW CAN I HELP, YOU KEEP TAKING BACK"...
"ALL THE THINGS THAT YOU WANT ME TO SEE?"...
"NOW THAT YOUR STUFF IS ALL IN MY HANDS"...
"YOURSELF, FAMILY AND FRIENDS IN THERE TOO"...
"BECAUSE YOU'LL HAVE NO NEED TO WORRY"...
"IF YOU JUST LET <u>ME</u> HOLD <u>ALL OF YOU</u>"...
"GET READY TO LET <u>ME</u> TAKE OVER"...
"MY HAND'S BIG ENOUGH FOR THE RIDE"...
"MY FINGERS ARE CLOSING AND TAKING YOUR CARES"...
"WORRIES AND SECRETS CAN'T HIDE"...
"<u>NOW, LEAVE THEM WITH ME AND REMEMBER</u>"...
"I'M BIGGER THAN YOU EVER KNEW"...
"I SAID THAT I ALWAYS WOULD BE HERE"...
"<u>MY HANDS WILL ALWAYS HOLD YOU</u>"...

Written by Margaret Bergeron October 2006

FROM SHABBY TO CHIC...

Picture the word "Shabby"...
You may think of tattered clothes...
Maybe just a messy house...
Or a hat with a wilted rose...

"Chic" is quite the opposite...
All dignity and grace...
Pictures from Vogue magazine...
Dressed up with painted face...

"Shabby" is your old life...
"Your own" footprints in the sand...
"Chic" is "Our Lord" holding you...
In the Palm of His Great Hand...

God made us all so perfect...
Like the finest silver vase...
Made our hearts like shining jewels...
With a fragile human case...

Close your eyes and ask yourself...
"Is your heart tattered and torn?"...
"Have you given your all to Him?"...
"To be polished, shined, adorned?"...

It's not too late to be shined up...
Trade in that "Shabby" shell...
Welcome "HE" that blesses you...
"Chic" will suit you well...

Written By Margaret Bergeron...2005

REWIND...

If you could just rewind some things...
That you regret you did...
Use a big remote control...
Undo something you hid...

Take back a word, a thought a time...
Go back to another day...
Undo the hurt you've brought to one...
Make it go away...

If someone would take back the words...
That hurt you way back when...
How would you feel about yourself...?
Would you feel whole again...?

If someone would say "I'm sorry"...
For all the wrong they've done...
Would it make it go away...?
Could your life be a better one...?

Yesterday has come and gone...
You only have today...
There is no "rewind" button...
To make it go away...

But you can still begin again...
Forgive and start anew...
Today is a new beginning...
It can be a "rewind" for you...

Written by Margaret Bergeron
January 2006

OH LORD, BLESS MY EARS…

Oh Lord Bless my ears…
I'm having a difficult time…
Hearing what the doctor says…
Can't hear the reason or rhyme…

It's hard to hear the telephone…
These ears are getting weak…
I strain to hear in restaurants…
And when my family speaks…

When I turned up my hearing aid…
Thought I would surely shriek…
The noise blasted back at me…
My ears hurt for a week…

Sometimes I have to turn it off…
Because it "wallows" so…
Everyone can hear the wails…
When my aid for hearing, blows…

Medicare is great and all…
But we don't get the best…
Hearing aids are cheap for us…
But they are worse than all the rest…

The good ones cost a fortune…
But at least your ears can hear…
Of course it takes some saving…
Like months or even years…

So I will be content for now…
With what I have been given…
So please be patient with me today…
I can't hear, but I'm still livin'…!

Written and Composed by Margaret Bergeron
June 2006

PLEASE BLESS IT ALL...

I told You not too long ago...
That our ears need to be blessed...
But then I got to thinking...?
What about the rest...?
If, our ears were the "ONLY" part...
That we prayed would somehow heal...
Then, how about our eyes and minds...?
Our knees, our arms, our feel...?
Sure, we might hear it all again...
Everything would be more clear...
But then our dimming eyes would say...
"Don't forget about "US" here...
So bless our eyes and while You're close...
Bless our noses and guard our mouth...
Our noses out of each other's way...
Our tongues from wagging south...!
We can't forget about our brain...
Because, "it's" forgetting so much...
Let us remember what matters most...
Always knowing a loved one's touch...
We could go down our bodies...
Listing joints that are feeling such pain...
Fingers and backs, hips and toes...
Especially, when there's rain...
You know about these ups and downs...
You know how to make pain ease...
Keep us from complaining much too much...
Won't You help us, Please...?
There are many parts to our bodies...
That need YOUR help, we pray...
First our ears and now our eyes...
"Something else" on another day...
Not asking for a newer model...
Just a little more pep would do...
Mend these worn out bodies of ours...
'Til its time to come see You...

Written by Margaret Bergeron
July 2006

144

PLEASE HELP US THIS DAY...

I'm sitting here alone again...Alone, just You and me...
Trying to pray for everything...That you would have me see...
I try so hard to know just what...You would have me do...
Looking all around Your world...So much must DIS-please You...
What happened to respect for all...?The people that provide...
The ones who make decisions for us...Whose laws, we should abide...?
So many children all mixed up...Not knowing just how to live...
Parents losing their control...How much leeway should they give...
Music, T.V., computers, phones...Yes, they have their place...
But why are wrong things thrown at us...And put up to our face...?
The way we drive each other nuts...The words that are exchanged...
The times we spend in anger...Lord, help us re-arrange...
We know you need our help with all...The problems in Your world...
Missionaries need support...So their lives will not unfurl...
The ones around us need our help...I'm sure You want us to...
Pray that everyone they teach... is ...Brought directly to You...!
You give us all the tools we need...In abundance, You have given...
All the things to help each other...For Your purpose, we're still livin'...
So, Lord, open my eyes this day...'Cause this is just the start...
Of how we should direct our prayers...Help to prepare our hearts...

Written by Margaret Bergeron
2007

SUMMERTIME...ALL THE TIME...

All of a sudden its Summertime...
The sun comes up so hot...
The stores sell watermelons...
And they don't cost a lot...
The beach is full of surfers...
And bathers on the sand...
Picnic baskets, ice cream cones...
Hikers enjoy our land...

Search for shells and driftwood...
Walk for miles and miles...
No real destination...
Loving the ocean smells...
Spectacular morning sunrise...
Our sunsets are sublime...
California summers are...
Twelve months of the time!!!

California has it all combined...
Instead of different seasons...
We have rain and sunny too...
While the other states are freezin'...
Don't get me wrong...(we have our FAULTS)...
Going up and down our coast...
Californians like surprise...
Just a little more than most!...

Look out at our ocean...
How the mountains kiss the seas...
Deserts hug the rivers...
Snowing or palm trees...
We have it all beside us...
Right where we belong...
Best-est weather in all the world...
Its Summertime all year long...!!!

Written by Margaret Bergeron
June 1998

BEING ROBBED

Its like someone else is living here...
That doesn't even belong...
Like having your home invaded...
I hope it won't last long...
At first we thought... - "It is the worst... "
"Thing...that could ever be"...
We lived inside just trembling...
"Why did it happen to me"...?

When someone takes your things away...
Only junk is left inside...
They break and batter all you have...
Nothing much is left besides...
There's one thing that they didn't take...
And this is what we kept...
Our Love & Faith & Honesty...
Although we truly wept...

Our family is safe, our house not burned...
Although it sure was messed...
God kept us away---just long enough...
We four were really blessed...
We learned a hard, hard lesson...
"In losing all we had"...
If we ever lost our love inside...
Then THAT would sure be sad...

Material things are great to have...
But if your heart is bare...
There'd be nothing left to pick you up...
You need some love to share...
The people that steal and rob from us...
Let them be guided too...
Lead them to right...away from crime...
And let it begin with you...

Written by Margaret Bergeron
February 1979

NEVER TO RETURN...

You left your homes to get away...
From wind and flood and waves...
Leaving behind all that you had...
Others hoping to be saved...
What must have felt like a lifetime...
Those hours and days that passed...
For so many people that were loved...
It was to be their last...
It's not just THINGS you left that day...
Your pets your homes your life...
Some of you even lost families...
Children, husbands, wives...
Neighborhoods and neighbors...
Friends scattered all around...
Some had to go to different states...
SOME never to be found...
You never could believe it would...
Turn out like this, for sure...
And NEVER TO RETURN BACK HOME...
Does not seem like a cure...
So now the water has gone down...
But lives are still misplaced...
The streets and towns, they still remain...
But the homes have been erased...
How can you deal with so much loss...?
Now where will your life be...?
There's SOMEONE BIGGER than all your loss...
Much BIGGER than you or me...
You must just feel so hopeless...
Where will your family go...?
Trust THE ONE who can carry you...
OUR LORD JESUS LOVES YOU SO-O-O...

Written by Margaret Bergeron
February 2006

LOOKING AT THE MOUNTAINS...

Going through the valley...
With desert all around...
Where the splendor of the mountains...
Can finally be found...
They almost look like mansions...
With all the hidden towers...
Spreading through the rocks and trees...
In awe of them for hours...

Some are so majestic...
God placed them way up high...
The smaller ones fill in the gaps...
Together, they make you sigh...
Every mountain is different...
Not one looks the same...
That's why some people took the time...
To give each one a name...

How could someone sit and gaze...
Upon a mountain top...
And not think of the Sculptor...
Because the beauty does not stop...
Not only just the mountains...
But the trees all green and gold...
The cows and horses stand around...
A vision to behold...

Does everyone feel little...?
Being on the ground...?
As we wander down the highway...
With the mountains all around...?
If God could make these giant peaks...
And place them so carefully...
How much more do you think He loves...
And cares for you and me...?

Written By Margaret Bergeron
July 2001

I'M NOT DONE NEEDING YOU YET...

We never really lose the need...When we love someone so deep...
Parents, children, our best friends...
Brothers and sisters can make us weep...

Sometimes they live nearby to us...Or sadly, far away...
Or when they go to meet Our Lord...There is happy and sad every day...

We cannot control what will happen...To those that we love so much...
A pet, a friend or family...Or the hundreds of lives they have touched...

So when you feel that you're not done...Needing someone just yet...
Remember the love that person has given...Is the daily blessing you get...

So whether you're needed or needy...There's something to do everyday...
Hold them close to your heart and your mind...
And keep holding them tight while you pray...

Whenever you feel you cannot get through...
You surely can make a bet...
It's not that YOU CAN'T MAKE IT THROUGH...
"You just are not done needing them yet..."

You never stop needing a loved one...Whether here, or so far away...
It comes from the Love God has shown us...
It is here AND IT'S NOT GOING AWAY...

Written by Margaret Bergeron
May 2006

I DO NOT MEAN TO HURT YOU...

How could I ever hurt you...?
You mean the world to me...
I'm sorry if I made you feel...
Less, than you should ever be...

I didn't mean to tell you...
"You said that once before"...
Or, "Did you forget, I told you"...
Or, "You forgot to close the door"...

I guess I did not realize...
That it hurts you when I say...
"Take my arm, let me help you"...
Though, I don't mean it THAT way...

It only means, "I Love You"...
"I want to help take care"...
Of all your needs and wants and mostly...
To always, for you, be there...

So, if I get impatient...
When you ask a question or two...
Reminding me to do something...
That I "promised" I'd try to do...

I only meant to love you...
Not to hurt you in any way...
I only want the best for you...
Every single day...

Written By Margaret Bergeron
October 8, 2001

HOW MUCH I LOVE YOU...

If you knew how much I love you...Then you'd trust the words I say...
You'd be walking with ME and listening...Every single day...

If only you could see from here...Just what I see in you...
Asking for forgiveness is...All you have to do...

If... you only knew how much...I love your perfect face...
Your bodies I made different...But, My love is evenly placed...

Some are strong and some are weak...You all have different needs...
Help each other where you can...If you're rich, let go of greed...

If you need some extra help...Don't be afraid to ask...
I promise I will help you...I can do the largest task...

If you only knew I'm waiting ...To help in every way...
How many times you fail to ask...I have SO much I want to say...

I WANT you to be prosperous...To be healthy, happy, fun...
Just put Me on your guest list...As the Most Important One...

If you only knew how many...Days I wait for you...
Hoping that tonight's the night...That you invite Me too...

I've been here since before your birth...With your name upon My Heart...
Guiding you to come to Me...Maybe today you'll start...

If you only knew I'm waiting...I'll be here 'til your last sigh...
Don't take too long to answer Me...
You'll FINALLY know just why...!
GOD...

Written by Margaret Bergeron
December 2006

LOVE...THE GREATEST GIFT OF ALL...

We're taught that we must speak our words...With love to everyone...
No matter who we're talking to...Everyone, means everyone...
If you have a gift to share...To help another grow...
Make sure that love is tucked inside...And let that person know...

We learn that Patience, is indeed...A virtue linked to Love...
Because Love tries our Patience...And Patience completes our Love...
Loves <u>kindness</u> touches all of us...<u>Love,</u> "envy" <u>does not know...</u>
Where there's Love, the "Green Eyed Monster"...Has <u>no</u> place he can go...

When you have Love, you do not brag...Or tell the world "you're it"...
Because you share your every gift...And you don't mind a bit...
Compassion rules out anger...No "record of others' wrongs"...
God takes care of vengeance...That's where our Faith belongs...

When we rejoice in truth and facts...We know that Love is there...
But when we hide from what is true...We think that Love's not fair...
When we protect our loved ones...Taking care to guard, until...
We trust that no more harm will come...<u>That's</u> loving with God's Will...

When we have Hope, combined with Love...Instead of despair and tears...
Our Faith can shine for all to see...To drive away all fears...
And Perseverance, simply means...To keep steady, strong and true...
For God is holding out His Hand...And gently guiding you...

We're given these virtues all our life...Never
knowing how much they mean...
Living and going about our days...Since we were only teens...
Many stages in each year...Never knowing where to go...
Sometimes taking wrong paths...Places we should never go...

And there's His Hand reaching out again...Forgiving, with such concern...
Waiting for us to finally change...A lesson we've almost learned...
We climb so many mountains...And many years we've roamed...
Until we find the right one...And then we find our Home...

Then the road seems paved and straight...Walking towards God above...
He gave us Faith and Hope and Love...But the greatest of these is LOVE...

Written by Margaret Bergeron...2008

DECISIONS....

Sitting in my car...
Not wanting to go in...
Knowing I'll disappoint one...
Either way, I cannot win...

Wish it could be different...
That was then, not now...
Many things have changed for me...
Can't really explain how...

Thought that I belonged here...
Had a great time too...
Learned a lot, and on the way...
Made friends with all of you...

But, now I need to start again...
To find a niche for me...
Being a "people pleaser"...
Is something hard to be...

Please understand my reasons...
I'm doing all I can...
To satisfy my heart and mind...
And follow a different plan...

I appreciate your help so much...
I'll remember you, so you know...
I couldn't and wouldn't forget you...
But, now I have to go...

Written by Margaret Bergeron
July 2001

BLESS, TO BE A BLESSING...

Bless to be a blessing...
Is what we ought to do...
Because each time you bless someone...
Blessings come and bless you too...

It may be someone you don't know...
Who doesn't know what to do...
Needing a little gentle touch...
With just one word from you...

You never know how just one word...
Can make some person's day...
It may not seem so much to you...
But it could light another's way...

Bring peace to everyone you meet...
Smile, to help their pain...
Hold their hand, heal their fears...
Give shelter if it rains...

Sometimes your light can change the dark...
Of someone's crumbling life...
Help to soothe a battered soul...
Or save them from some strife...

Christmas is over, the lights come down...
But don't put CHRISTMAS away...
Christmas lives in all our lives...
Every single day...

So, Bless, to be a blessing...
And watch what happens to you...
Blessings will overfill their hearts...
And will spill right on to you...

Written by Margaret Bergeron
December 2007

SURFER BOY...

He is the handsome Surfer Boy...That captured your young heart...
The moment that you saw him...You knew it was the start..
You watched him in the ocean....from the moment he went in...
With all the other surfers...You always could see him...
Just the way he paddled...The "goofy" way he put his toes...
The strength and beauty of his back...Hanging
"ten" on the surfboard's nose...
You waited for him endlessly...In cold, or wind or rain...
Even as his lips turned blue...He never seemed to feel the pain...

Is it "yet" six foot and glassy...?Do you feel an "offshore" wind...?
Was it "Victory at Sea"...?Has it "turned to mush" again...?
Whether it is at "Old Mans"..."18's" or at the "Tank"...
Catching waves, no matter where...It is "Dear God" you thank...
It's been over forty years...We've watched waves come and go...
Our "Dear Surfer Men" were "boys"...Oh, so long ago...
(Our "Dear Surfer Men" are still "boys"...)
(And we have many years to go...!)

Funny, how we thought surfing...Was just a "passing craze"...
One day "they" would just "grow up"...Forget their silly ways...
Remember, standing on the shore...Watching our "Surfer Boys"...
Thinking "soon", it would be done...They'd go on to "bigger toys"...
It truly is a blessing...When we watch them paddle out...
We don't <u>even</u> have to wonder...What it is they talk about...
Even though the "times" have changed...They're wearing "wetsuits" too...
Boards are still long, but lighter...Their lips, no longer blue...

A few more aches and pains today...Than all those years ago...
But they say its worth it...As they wax their "sticks" and go...!
We've all been friends for many years...We all go way, way back...
Remember tightening those straps...Of the old time "surfing racks...?
To our "Special Surfer Boys"...We "Girls" are women now...
Inside, we still feel seventeen...You've kept us young, somehow...
As I look out at the ocean...Through all the waves and sand...
I see all of our faces...Friendships, and fun we've had...
So, don't change a thing for us...Promise you'll stay the same...
"Surfer Boy" or "Surfer Men"...Will always be your names...

Written by Margaret Bergeron...Especially for
Bill, Gilbert and Tom ... July 1999

SO MUCH TO SAY TO YOU...

So much to say about you love... On your arm I feel complete...
You still can give me goose bumps... From my head down to my feet...

"44" years ago we met...Been engaged for 43...
Married 42 years ago next month... And I'm HAPPY AS I COULD BE...

God has been so good to us... We never have been needy...
Making us truly grateful... Not letting us be greedy...

It is true, we've had some ups & downs... But that is nothing new...
The best part of disagreeing... Is making up with you...

We've traveled and made memories... Since 1967...
We've raised two gorgeous babies... On loan to us from heaven...

We've been awarded grandkids...That we love 'til our hearts could burst...
Being a grandparent is so much fun...We should have had them first...

Surfing was your passion... It became routine for us...
I brought the chicken and chocolate cake...
And you brought "me", that's a plus...

For hours I would wait and shiver...As the fog and the wind filled the sky...
You would come out and eat all the lunch...
Go back in...and I'd wonder why...?

At first, I thought, "this is a phase"... "Surely something you'd outgrow"...
How could I know then, that you never will...
"You still love that big ocean so"....

A part of your charm, I saw long ago... While
observing the look in your eye...
Gazing upon the waves and the surf...
God blessed me with "just the right guy"...

Written by Margaret
Just for Bill, my love forever ...April 1998 and 2009

ORANGE COUNTY HOME SHOW

We are very pleased to be...
A part of every day...
While your Show "exhibits"...
Home "fixin's" on display...
Seminars and information...
For all to share and do...
Make our homes look better...
Our "thanks" go out to you...
We're glad you read "The Mobile Home News"...
It has a lot to say...
About our parks and residents...
And what we do each day...
Many plan their potlucks...
Some play Bingo too...
Cards & billiards, social time...
It's always up to you...
Protected little communities..
Lined up in tidy rows...
Flower boxes and shutters...
Around our front windows...
Everybody waves a lot...
It's just the "thing" we do...
Mobile owners making sure...
No "trouble" coming through...!
Lots of signs in mobile parks...
"Speed limit", "Don't Park", "Conserve"...
"Children at Play", "Duck Crossings"...
"Slow Down", so you won't swerve...
Our close-knit style of living...
Puts our neighbors within reach...
It really is ideal (and plus)...
We live real near the beach...!!!
So, "thank you" to the HOME SHOW...
For sharing "US" this week...
For giving us some great ideas...
While letting our "newspaper" speak...

Written by Margaret Bergeron
August 1998

AFTER THE SHOW...

After the "SHOW" is over...
The garden and blooms disappear...
We'll say we had a good time, and...
Look forward to next year...

The moment that we had arrived...
We found we could not wait...
To see just what you had in store...
For us, behind the gate...

The planning of committees...
People, displays and food...
The crowds and smiling faces...
Created a happy mood...

You always do amaze us...
There's always more to see...
You never run out of "ideas"...
On how our homes "could" be...

We bought with "good" instruction...
Many "treasures" from the SHOW...
The specials and variety...
Get better each year that we go...!!

THANK YOU to THE HOME SHOW...
Your "Helpers, Committees and Crew"...
For all the many months of toil...
Our "Hats" go off to you...!!!!!

Written by Margaret Bergeron
August 1998

GOING AWAY

You all are moving far away...Back to Little Rock...
Brand new life for everyone...A "loss" for our little block...

Giving you "all" a bonding...To share love and hugs everyday...
Building a special relationship...While blending your lives on the way...

Feelings we have are "bittersweet"...Being happy and yet, sad...
We'll miss out on a lot of things...But we're grateful for all we've had...

Bunk beds are going with you...All the games and toys...
Countless little "treasures"...Belonging to "our" boys...

Like "2" gentle twisters...Swirling around our hearts...
Never knew what to expect...Missing you is just the start...

We HAVE to 'let you go again!...'"..It's not easy....But we'll see...
That giving you all some room to grow...Will make your lives happy...

We do not take it lightly...We know you feel the same...
Making a vow is a whole lot more...Than getting a brand new name...

A wonderful man has captured you...And stole your heart away...
To make you his beautiful "Mrs."...Forever and a day...

That is a real good reason...To pack up and get married too...
Knowing that your "dear Les"...Will take "real" good care of you...

We hope this little poem of ours...Has let you know just how...
A special occasion seems to be...That you're getting married now...
(Another good time to say... How very much, that you are loved...)

Mommy and Daddy too!
Written by Margaret Bergeron...1995

160

SKILL OF A SURGEON...

I surely cannot fathom...
How a surgeon knows...
How to go about repairing...
Our bodies...head to toes...
Have you ever thought about...
The skill of a surgeon's hand...?
How their mind and expertise...
Has your operation planned...

Where to start, what they think...
When they should be done...
How they know it's all okay...
Is performing surgery fun...?
Does it keep them up at night...
(Like it does for you)...
Is it just a job for them...
Or do they "feel" it too...?

Pick your surgeon very well...
Learn all there is to know...
After all, it is your body...
That they will cut and sew...!
Ask the questions, be exact...
Feel confident and sure...
The skill of your own surgeon...
Will let you be secure...
When surgery is finished...
When all the pain is nil...
When you are on the mend again...
Remember Your Surgeon's Skill...

Written by Margaret Bergeron
April 11, 2000

AROUND THE CORNER...

If we didn't turn around the corner...
Just think what we could miss,,,
Seeing Our Lord in a garden...
On a morning just like this...
Get up and pray for someone...
Don't let the moment go...
Pray for those around you...
Or, for those you do not know...
There will still be troubles...
That we will have to bear...
But God will never leave you...
He will still be there...

Equip yourself with blessings...
No matter what they are...
God has given <u>you</u> a gift...
You can be a shining star...
God will surely stir your nest...
Our resting place, our bed...
Giving us the wings to fly...
And "His Shoulder" to rest your head...
He will never let you fall...
His arms will hold you close...
"Be still and <u>know</u> that "HE" is God...
When your heart needs Him the most...

Whatever stirs in you right now...
Give it to God today...
You'll be surprised how He will take...
Your worries and cares away...

Written by Margaret Bergeron
May 17, 2003

IMPATIENCE

Looking at your wristwatch...
Ten times in a row...
Shows you how impatience...
Can mess your life up so...

Pacing back and forth in line...
Or waiting for a call...
Tapping fingers nervously...
Unwilling to wait at all...

Showing no compassion...
To those who show up late...
Making sure you're early...
For appointments or a date...

Making mental notes on how...
You think you could go faster...
Squeezing more into a day...
Could be a real disaster...

Heart is saying, "Please slow down"...
Bones cry, "Take a break"...
Lungs are starving, "Take a breath"...
"How much can they take...?"

Eyes are blinking, "Let me rest"...
Brain begs, "Please, no more"...
Mind and Body on overload...
Tired to the core...!

Must take time to re-assess...
Before you start out new...
Impatience can take over...
If you let it get to you...!

Written by Margaret Bergeron
September 1999

WHEN YOU THINK YOU CAN'T GO ON...

If you ever get the feeling...
That your life is just too much...
Many problems, many tasks...
That you feel out of touch...
Too many people leaning...
On your shoulders every day...
Then, sit right down and think about...
What "God" would have to say...
"I made you to be servants..."
"Only here for a little stay..."
"Your real home is in Heaven..."
"That's where your treasures lay..."
"Do each task in all your life..."
"With love and hope and care..."
"Giving all you have to give..."
"As if God were standing there..."
"Never let a day go by..."
"Without helping out someone..."
"You don't have to know them..."
"Your living will be more fun... "
"Say the best about your friends..."
"Boost them at every chance..."
"Make everyone feel special..."
"In every circumstance..."
"Keep the negative to yourself..."
"Keep it "far" from tongue or mouth..."
"Pretty soon, your life will change..."
"Bad feelings will go "south"..."
"If you could just remember"...
"How it is you like to feel"...
"Treat each other, just the same"...
"Build a friendship that is real"...
So, instead of thinking, "you can't go on"...
"Show love to one another"...
God made us all to serve Him...
Each person a sister and brother...

Written by Margaret Bergeron
November 2002

DEER...NEXT 14 MILES...

Do the deer know where to cross...?
Or where they're supposed to eat...?
Do they look for signs with "Deer"...?
Before they brave the street...?

Do they measure 14 miles...
And "can't" walk past the sign...
Do they know we're looking...
To see them "maybe" cross that line...?

Where are they when they "aren't" there...?
Do they hide to make us laugh...?
So ones like me can think of words...
To rhyme in a paragraph...?

So, if they stay between the signs...
And cross at the "Deer Cross" place...
Can Cows or Elk or Bears cross too...?
Or at some "other" place...?

Written by Margaret Bergeron
On a silly day
March 2003

IF YOUR HEART COULD TALK...

If your heart could talk to you...
What do you think it'd say...?
"Please, won't you take good care of me...?"
"Please, exercise each day...!"

"Swim and do deep breathing..."
"Eat lots of leafy greens..."
"Sleep eight hours every night..."
"Don't treat each other mean..."

"Smile at every chance you have..."
"And, pray...unceasingly..."
"Hug your loved ones all the time..."
"Care for everyone you see..."

"Sing, at least once daily..."
"Cry, when you have to..."
"Love each other with a smile..."
"A happy heart will service you..."

"If your heart could talk to you..."
"Just think how well you'd be..."
"You'd never light a cigarette..."
"Less coffee, you'd have tea..."

"Heartache wouldn't hurt so bad..."
"Love would be more true..."
"Everyone would give a smile..."
"Right on back to you..."

Your heart might say, "Enjoy your life..."
"Don't worry every day..."
"Live each day like it's your last..."
That's what your heart would say...!

Written by Margaret Bergeron
June 2003

JUST TRUST ME...

Whenever you think you can't go on...
JUST TRUST ME...

When the storm is just too big...
FEEL ME...

When the pain is oh, so deep...
CALL ME...

When calm has come at last...
REMEMBER ME...

-GOD-

Written by Margaret Bergeron
May 17, 2003

LOYALTY...

Where did all the flags go...?
They flew most everywhere...
Clamped to windows of our cars...
When they broke, we had a spare...
Selling on street corners...
So we could show how proud...
We feel about our country...
We "supported" it out loud...

Stood behind our President...
And all he gets us through...
Instead of holding protest signs...
We should hug the "red, white and blue"...
Show support for all our Troops...
Whatever they MUST do...
Instead of sitting in the street...
Making a fool of you...

Our flag STILL stands for Freedom...
And war is STILL a shame...
Soldiers STILL have fought for us...
The outcome STILL the same...
They're fighting for OUR FREEDOM...
Not because they want to kill...
Making sure our families...
Can have a life here...STILL....

We elect a leader...
God guides his every move...
So, unless you want the job yourself...
What does protesting prove...?
If you've had a life oppressed...
You'd appreciate being free...
Hold a flag up to our President...
He is working for you and me...

Written by Margaret Bergeron
March 2003

SMILE AT YOUR FUTURE

Wonder how this young girl... Not even "planned" to be...
Stayed alive despite the odds... She claimed her destiny...

She endured such torment... Through rape, abuse and pain...
She still forgave and cared for all... Her hardship was her gain...

Seemed, the worse they treated her... Instilled a stronger will...
Taking care of everyone... And a little girl...still...

Surviving her step-father's fury... Nursed her mother's sickness too...
Endured her horrid grandmother...But her dream was coming true...

She worked so hard for freedom... And finally, came the day...
She did not know the language... Or a soul in the USA...

But a fighter and determined... Claimed her place and made the best...
Of all that life could offer... And put aside the rest...

Found her way to New York State... Working more than sleep...
Making friends that made her smile... And a way of life to keep...

This book will show forgiveness... Makes you want to hug her heart...
Made her life so full of love... When it could have been torn apart...

For Wanka was not wanted... But "that" was not to be...
Becoming everything "good" instead... A surprise, as you will see...

Makes you think, could this be real...? Was there such a girl as this...?
How could she overcome such strife...? Its a life you won't dismiss...

Written by Margaret A. Bergeron
For the inside flap of Sonita DeLa Barca's book "WANKA"...
October 2000

LITTER ON THE ROADSIDE...

I'm the litter on the roadside...
No place I can go...
You throw me out the window...
So all I do is blow...

Messing up the hillside...
Streets and freeways too...
Only way that it will stop...
Begins and ends with you...

Only takes a second...
To put me in the trash...
Keep a bag inside your car...
Don't flick a butt or ash...

If everyone would do their part...
To keep our roadside clean...
Then I would have a place to go...
Not part of the freeway scene...

Written by Margaret Bergeron
March 2003

RECOVERY...

Realize that only God...
Can have power in your life...
Really know that He's in charge...
Don't be fooled by your own strife...
Earnestly believe that God exists...
That YOU really matter to Him...
Only He can give the help...
To get you off that limb...
Consciously choose to commit your life...
Your control, and will and all...
Christ is waiting this very day...
For your desperate call...
Openly confess your faults...
To yourself and a trusted friend...
Confess your life and heart to God...
He's with you 'til the end...
Voluntarily submit to change...
That He requests of you...
Ask Him to remove for good...
Defects and deep hurts too...
Evaluate your relationships...
Stay around people that care...
Pray for friends and enemies...
Give thanks...God's always there...
Reserve a daily time with God...
Meditate on all His ways..
Let Him lead you from temptation...
Guiding you through your days...
Yearn for every blessing...
While letting go of pain...
Open up your heart and soul...
Be cleansed by God's healing rain...
Tears, as well as happiness...
Can help you to recover...
Just remember who's in charge...
He'll heal you like no other...

Written by Margaret Bergeron
March 27, 2000

THE RAIN...

Something that we need so much...
Sure can make a mess...
It fills our aqueducts and dams...
But rain can cause much stress...
To everyone it's different...
Depends to whom you speak...
Some would like the rain to last...
Week after week, after week...
Some stay in their houses...
Waiting for it to subside...
Others don't drive in the rain...
They'd rather catch a ride...
Some have been in accidents...
Or trapped within a car...
People all have fears from rain...
Just depends on who you are...
Rain can be a comfort...
If you're cozy, safe and sound...
Warm socks on and jammies...
And familiar things around...
As long as everyone you love...
Is home and cozy too...
You can then relax awhile...
No rain will get to you...
Rain can be a nuisance...
Flooding out your roads...
Rocks & mud are fine in their place...
Not invading your abodes...
Then, it stops, the rainbow comes...
The air is sweet and fresh...
Puffy clouds just float away...
(You almost don't notice the mess)...
The sun, once again, comes out...
And everything's okay...
Life goes back to normal...
Until another rainy day...

Written by Margaret Bergeron
February 2000

A MAMMOGRAM...

A very sheepish subject...
All women will agree...
I'm sitting here in the waiting room...
Until they call for me...
You put it off and dread it...
Important...It is SO...
If they could make it faster...
And not squish us down so low...
I will just await my call...
And close my eyes real tight...
And pray to God that the results...
Will surely turn out right...
Everyone should have this test...
Once a year for sure...
It takes just minutes from your day...
And not TOO hard to endure...
We do this for each other...
No one likes this task...
Bare-ing everything we have...
Is sometimes a lot to ask...
But if we can be healthy...
To some degree, we hope...
Days would go more smoothly...
Helping us to cope...
Remember, as we're older...
A Mammogram is a test...and...
PREVENTION IS WORTH A POUND OF CURE...
In caring for your breasts...

Written by Margaret Bergeron...1996

IF WE HAD OUR WAY

When your family lives real far... Not just down the way...
Living in a different state... Can't drive in just a day...

It's then you start to realize... How you miss them all...
Especially at Christmas time.. You want more than just to call...

How you want them all to come... No matter what the price...
Pack the children and all of you... Then Christmas will be nice...

It used to be, in olden times... We all lived down the way...
Going out to lunch at noon... Home by dinner, the same day...

We send our gifts through UPS... And miss the hugs and smiles...
When friends and family move away... All those many miles...

If we had our druthers...We'd buy a plot of land...
Build houses for our families...Now, wouldn't that be grand...?

Help each other daily... And wave across the way...
Share our Sunday dinners... Less phone bills to pay...!

I have just been dreaming...It's not an easy task...
Moving loved ones and placing them... Isn't something we can ask...

But it's sure nice to think of it...No more aching heart...
If we lived near our families...We wouldn't be apart...

So if we had our way, right now...You'd be on your way...
But we will have to be content...To your visit another day...

Written by Margaret Bergeron
December 1999

A JOURNAL...

You should write a journal...
Write every day or night...
Feelings, hopes and happenings...
Put goals in your sight...
Write the things you're thankful for...
And things you can improve...
Write about the things you see...
Or a habit to remove...
Write about the weather...
Or where you went that day...
Write about a book you read...
Or something you will say...
Capture the many wonders...
Of what you saw today...
This is your own journal...
No rules, no special way...
Remember, as you're writing...
About life and what you do...
It will be another memory...
Of all that you've gone through...
Write memos to your loved ones...
So that it will be known...
How much you do appreciate...
The love and care they've shown...
Write about a friend who called...
Brightened your day with cheer...
You don't need any fancy words...
Your own are very clear...
I could go on and on...
And tell you every line...
But they would not be "your" thoughts...
The journal would be mine...
First thing that you need to do...
Find a special book and pen...
Start to write your thoughts and then...
Your "Journal" will begin...

Written by Margaret Bergeron –
October 20, 1999

A CABIN BY HIMSELF...

A country cabin by itself...
With two country cabin chairs...
All alone, just one old man...
With hardly any hair...

Sitting on his porch so long...
Time just passes by...
Never going anywhere...
Not ever knowing why...

Doesn't own a car or truck...
Just lives from day to day...
Happy, with a smile so big...
No frowns, no tears, no way...

Just a little slower now...
He doesn't have to hurry...
Lives his life so simply...
He doesn't even worry...

Every time he thinks of her...
Where she sat in the other chair...
He smiles an even bigger smile...
As if she was still there...

They shared a life so full of love...
Nothing could compare...
Except for, WHERE SHE WAITS FOR HIM...
And she's saving him a chair...

Written By Margaret Bergeron...1997

A CABIN BY HERSELF...

A country cabin by itself...
With two country cabin chairs...
All alone... a lovely lady...
With silver in her hair...

Sitting on her porch so long...
Time just passes by...
Never going anywhere...
Not ever knowing why...

Doesn't even own a car...
Just lives from day to day...
Happy, with a smile so big...
No frowns, no tears, no way...

Just a little slower now...
She doesn't have to hurry...
Lives her life so simply...
She doesn't even worry...

Every time she thinks of him...
Where he sat in the other chair...
She smiles an even bigger smile...
As if he was still there...

They shared a life so full of love...
Nothing could compare...
Except for, WHERE HE WAITS FOR HER...
And he's saving her a chair...

Written By Margaret Bergeron...1997

A CHRISTMAS TO REMEMBER...

Remember your favorite Christmas....?Close your eyes and try to see...
Was it a special present...?Underneath your Christmas tree...?

Was it your favorite cousins...?Grandpas or Grandmas...?
Or, the awe of tinsel and lights...?Or wearing new pajamas...?

Remembering Santa and his sleigh...Filled with so much stuff...
Closing your eyes, pretending...(Thinking you could call his bluff...)

Waiting till the sun came up...Waking your mom or dad...
Filled with such excitement...(Whether you were good or bad...)

Perhaps turkey and stuffing...?Or spicy pumpkin pie...?
Topped with fluffy whipping cream...?(Some memories make you cry...!)

The year you got your favorite doll...?Or the ring you dreamed about...?
A special visit from a friend...?You remember without a doubt...

One day you learned the reason...That we celebrate this day...
Jesus was born to save us...Honoring Him in a special way...

A Christmas to Remember, is...The one that makes us see...
That presents are fun and festive...But not ONLY what Christmas means...

As you look upon the manger...We see with our own eyes...
The KING who loves and died for us...To truly save our lives...

A Christmas to Remember...Is a perfect memory...
When we're gathered all together...Just God and you and me..

Written by Margaret Bergeron...1998

CASINO BOUND...

Get up real early...Wear comfortable shoes...
Bring all your coins...And money with you...
Go to the clubhouse...Waiting in line...
Time for a drink...You're feeling so fine...

Get to the freeway..."A dollar a card"...
Start playing Bingo...That's not so hard...
At the Casino...Where to go first...?
Keno or poker...?"Do you hunger or thirst"...?

Decide to play nickels...Then the quarters do call...
Dollar slots begging...Hear more money fall...
Getting your coins back...?By feeding them more...?
Minds are so crazy...But, who's keeping score...?

Just ONE more coin...Then you'll win the pot...!
Someone pulls the handle...Takes home all you brought...!
Time for a food break...Before cash $ is gone...
Fill up and relax ...Or we can't go on...

Time's almost over...Nearly BROKE to the core...
The big bus is waiting...We want to play more...!
One last machine...Calls out to you...
"Put money in me"...What else could you do...?

Only one nickel...You cannot say no...
You take a deep breath...'THREE 7's IN A ROW...!!!
INSTEAD of you winning...What THREE would bestow...
You won JUST a token...And now you MUST go...!

On the way home...Some winning... some not...
If you had MORE NICKELS...You'd have
SURELY WON THAT POT...!
So... until the next time...We'll save a little more...
Play a little smarter...To even up the score...!

Written by Margaret Bergeron...
February 2003

GOT FAITH ...?

We must RECEIVE the Word of Faith...
Tune in, Take Charge, Tone Down...
Be quick to listen, don't get mad...
Weed out Immoral ground...

We must REFLECT on the Word of Faith...
Read, Remember, Review...
Meditate on God's Word all day long...
Then use it in all that you do...

We must RESPOND to the Word of Faith...
By walking with God in all ways...
Keep a tight reign on words from your mouth...
God's blessings will blanket your days...

TEMPTATION is ever present in life...
But God NEVER prompts us at all...
It is our own CHOICE to give in to sin...
Just LEARN TO SAY NO and don't fall...

FAITH is believing that God will be there...
Even though, you have not seen His face...
FAITH is just knowing it will be okay...
No matter what time or what place...

Make everyday, just for THE LORD...
Never forget... He is here...
Give all your worries and doubts to Our God...
You'll forget that you had any fear...

At night when you rest, give all of your Thanks...
REMEMBER to give Him your all...
Then you will see, you will surely have FAITH...
On Jesus, you ALWAYS can call...

Written by Margaret Bergeron
February 2003

WANDER TOGETHER...

Wander with me to the ocean...
Where water and sky meet the sand...
Let's go on a journey together...
Come, won't you please take my hand...?
Let's wander to places...Where we've been in our minds...
Where happiness takes us...To help us unwind...
A place on the mountaintop...That let's us see far...
The deserts or valleys...Forget who we are...
A place we feel safe...Like a hug from a friend...
Somewhere that there is no...Beginning or end...
Where we can just wander...Smell flowers or grass...
Stroll down a path...Walk slow, or walk fast...
Meet someone special...Embrace, hug and smile...
Have tea with a neighbor...Just wander awhile...
Go on a journey...Without going too far...
Just stay where we wander...Don't go in a car...
We can wander around...Our yard or our home...
Just thinking about...All the hours to roam...
There are prayers we can pray...And songs we could sing...
Words we could write...And good things to bring...
All the places we go...Could bring us such joy...
Just forget how we got there...There's a path, don't be coy...
The path is a short one...Or as long as we please...
Take a moment to wander...We can reach it with ease...
It's just any place...We feel safe and secure...
That place in our hearts...It's in us...I'm sure...
Let's try to go often...Each day for a bit...
Bask in the feeling...Relax, smile, just sit...
Be still and just listen...God is wandering too...
Be still and just hear Him...He will listen to you ...

Written by Margaret Bergeron...1996

A PILL...

A pill for that old shoulder...Another for the pain...
A tablet for the stubborn aches...When our forecast is for rain...
And when you feel depressed and sad...We have a pill for that...
Also if you're full of stress...There's even one to heal the cat...
If we get a real sore throat...Or a cough, we get some spray...
Our ears are plugged and so we get...Some drops 4 times a day...
And now they have some special swabs...To use before you're sick...
You put it in your "almost" sick nose...It's on a q-tip stick...
And if you are around someone...That sneezed or coughed on you...
There is a fizzy drink you mix ...To keep from getting sick too...!
Drink lots of water and Vitamin C...Get sleep and stay away...
From all the people sick with stuff...That could sure ruin your day...
And if you're feeling pudgy...You wouldn't want to fret...
When you want to lose weight fast...There's another one for that...
And if your heart beats a little fast...If hot flashes make you drown...
Or if your thyroids fast or slow...There's more to swallow down...
And what about the headaches...?Is it sinus or migraine...?
Perhaps you've trouble sleeping...Or can't wake up again...!
There's bad knee pain, back pain too...Your feet they swell or tingle...
There's a pill for all these things...And something in the middle...
Your eyes are feeling a bit dry...Or tearing a bit too much...
Some drops or pills will help you out...With just a single touch...
Your fingers ache and get all numb...You'd better call the doc...
He'll write you a prescription...Or prescribe some type of shot...
Your blood pressure is rising...Your cholesterol is sky high...
There is a pill to lower both...So you can breathe a sigh...
And if you have diarrhea...Or the opposite is true...
There's just the pill for you to take...It will work real good for you...
So think of anything that hurts...Or aches or throbs with pain...
Or tingles, numb or stabs in places...Or comes and goes with rain...
Or when you cannot think of things...When you life's out of control...
Remember there's a name for it...And a pill to make you whole...
What happened to relax and pray...?Walk or swim in the pool...?
Stretch those legs and eating right...A hobby, go to church or school...?
There're pills we need and that's for sure...They get us through the day...
But one for EVERY symptom...Can take your life away...!
We must be able to feel some pain...Or stress or aches or strife...
Cause if we numbed our every day...We couldn't experience life...
Of course there're things that we must take...To let us live with ease...
Just don't mix up the "feel good drugs"...As a substitute for these...!

Written by Margaret Bergeron
2006

LITTLE DID YOU KNOW...

How could you ever make it...?
Without the love they give...?
These past few years have been the best...
That you could ever live...

Oh, sure, you've had some problems...
That sure could fill a book...!
But with their help and encouragement...
Plus, their love...is all it took...!

Little did you know...
They'd be such major parts...
Of all your daily prayers and plans...
And a big part of your hearts...

You thank them for their loving ways...
You thank them for their care...
God Bless them for their GIVING Souls...
And for ALWAYS being there...

Little did you know...
That God would guide you to this group...
While urging you to grow...
Show how you need each other...
But the need for God to show...
How much you must rely on Him...
Little did you know...

Written by Margaret Bergeron
September 2004

EMPTY OLD CAFÉ...

How many folks have shared a meal...?
And their stories along the way...
Sat each day with loved ones...
In that empty old café...

Chairs and tables still the same...
Like way back in its day...
Dusty worn out curtains...
In that empty old café...

Many laughs and friends were heard...
Drinking coffee, with a sigh...
Comfort foods, like stew and soup...
And that special apple pie...!

Twinkle lights were on all year...
Then they closed it one sad day...
That's when all the life went out...
Of that empty old café...

So there it stays, with all its charm...
Like a safe place, way back then...
The empty old café remains...
Keeping all the memories in...

Walk by just to look at it...
Where are the people though...?
The empty old café still stands...
And you sure miss it so...

Written by Margaret Bergeron
April 2004

MOM AND DAD "70" YEARS...!

This poem is just for you...I'll probably make it rhyme...
It could be hard for me to read...So, give me a little time...
It all started with a single rose...That he placed upon her desk...
The card said only.. "Johnny"...And here's what happened next...
They got married at an early age...To love forever and a day...
Share their life and vows they made...Have children, watch them play...
SO THAT IS WHAT THEY DID...
Mom and Dad, you gave us life...You've given your best to us...
We didn't listen all the time...But we never heard you cuss...
You taught us, belief and trust in God...You showed us, love and care...
You gave us understanding...You were always, always there...
Dad always teased and joked a lot...His smile, a treat to see...
You labeled a bullet, and scared a few...But that was to protect...me...
And Mom still worries all the time...About friends and family too...
We know things wouldn't go so well...If it were not for all you do...
You've really kept together...Our family and our ties...
The job you've both done deserves applause...How did you get so wise...?
We know Mom's cooking is the best...Ask everyone that knows...
For the greatest place to eat in town... It's to... Grandma's house we go...!
And, even Dad's cooking can't be beat...Have you ever tried his beans...?
As long as he's got some BACON to use...And OKRA as the greens...
We've all had ups and downs in life...And gone through many ages...
Our bond with you both, will always he...What got us through those stages...
We had a celebration for your 60th...Ten whole years ago...
You both keep getting better...Dearer as you grow...
Now you're married 70 years...You can still make each other smile...
They smile a certain way, that's shows...They've loved for quite awhile...
A lot has happened in all those years...Some lives have passed away...
But I'll just bet they're all here...Smiling on this special day...
And a lot of loved ones added...To your growing family tree...
Married grandchildren and more being born...A delight for you to see...
70 years ago this day...You vowed your love together...
There 's been some sickness and poorer...But a good mixture of "better"...
You've been blessed with grandkids...And great-grandkids as well..
Neither one of you look old enough...No one could ever tell....
Of course, you both must know by now...No one could ever take your places...
Loving you for all of these years...We've grown accustomed to your faces...
Through all the fun and hardships...Through all the smiles or tears...
Still touching the hearts that love you...For all these many years...
So, Mom this is "YOUR" day...We hope you'll always know...and Dad,
How very much we love you...And appreciate you so...!!!!
HAPPY" 70 "ANNIVERSARY MOM AND DAD...2009

MOTHER MARY GEMMA...

Mother Gemma, you're the one...That shines out in the crowd...
To say that you once taught us...Makes us very proud...
There's a special reason for this day...A most important matter...
It comes from all her "dearest" friends...And all of us that had her...
She's just the type to strive to do...The things that mean so much...
She's always there to help you out...She has that special touch...
She seems to know your every thought...As if it were hers too...
You think she may not show it...But she knows the things we do...

Whenever you have joys to share...She seems to glow inside...
She even cries when you are sad...Her feelings she can't hide...
Understanding was another trait...That she could hold up high...
Every heart was mended...And problems just whizzed by...
Sometimes she tried so extra hard...To make the day just right...
For instance, our class picnic...And graduation night...
No matter what the subject was...She gave a goal to reach...
In schoolwork, boy, she knew her books....
Mother Gemma could really teach...

Her students seemed to want to do...The things that made her smile...
From '58 to '64...Their efforts were worthwhile...
We never ever will forget ...The joy she seemed to give...
No matter where her path may turn...Her memories will always live...
The convent just won't be the same...That's what the Sisters say...
It'll have to take her double...To brighten up their day...
A sparkling gem to her loved ones...True green in her Irish Home Town...
As pure as snow to God...She'd never let you down...

And so, Dear Mother Gemma...The time has come to part...
We hope that you'll be happy there... And keep us in your heart...
We hope this day for you has been...A memorable one...
We're hoping that you'll look back...And think of all the fun...
May God be with you at every step...As you enter your new home...
May your every thought be happy...As you read back through this poem...
Think about us often...Keep us in your prayers...
And when you're feeling lonely...Remember "Saint James" cares...
Farewell Party...Saint James School... 1958-1964

Written by Margaret "McClinton" Bergeron
1964

CARI LYNNE...

Seem like yesterday you were little...
You couldn't reach me at all...
You'd wear my nightgown and Daddy's boots...
Prancing down the hail...

Records of Rick Springfield...
That's all you wanted to hear...
Slumber parties and ice cream...
Traded for pizza and beer...

All of a sudden it happens...
We were unaware...
Cari's no longer the baby...
Entrusted to our care...

She now has children of her own...
(Of which we get to boast)...
But, they live "too" far away...
Arkansas' not near our coast...

She needs some "gentle" persuasion...
To pack her bags again...
To say good-bye to Little Rock...
From...tornadoes. wind and rain...

We just miss y'all so much...
Life is just not as fun...
Our children close to us...
In the California sun...
(Won't you at least think about it???)...

We love you, Mom and Dad...
May 1997

CHRISTMAS TIME...

Christmas day is once a year...Sometimes you're really glad...
Because of all the shopping...With money that you HAD...
The parties and the cooking...With family, neighbors, friends...
Dressing up and stepping out...You "sometimes" wish it wouldn't end...
Making plans and off you go...With lists to shop all day...
Returning, pooped with tired face...Is there another way...?
The day is close, much left to do...How will it all get done...?
Sometimes even forgetting about...The most "Important One"...
Big trees with bulbs and twinkle lights... Christmastime is near...
Getting together to share our love... God's blessings are truly here...
The Reason for the Season...Is the birth of God's own Son...
Remember when we're shopping...Buying gifts for everyone...
Hopefully we'll think about...Thanking Him every day...
For all our friends and family...And our neighbors down the way...
For all the freedom given us...In this world that He has made...
For hearts that feel and love and give...For all the plans He laid...
Let's thank Him for our ups and downs...For funny, laughs and smiles...
For food upon our table...And making life worthwhile...
And when we look up in the sky...For clouds and moon and sun...
Stars and rain and seldom snow... Caring especially for someone...
For making our great country...Brave and strong and wise...
For all these years with Santa Claus...With his big blue twinkling eyes...
For children and grandbabies...With their eyes so full of awe...
As they finally get their presents...From Grandma and Grandpa...
For our health and independence...As long as you give us, here...
We'll keep on saying "thank You"...Year after year, after year...
Dear God, bless EVERYONE here today...As we gather all together...
Keep us all in the Palm of Your Hand...
And, "Thank you for our wonderful weather!!!"...

Written by Margaret Bergeron
2003

MY DAUGHTER...

Can't begin to tell you...
What I feel right now...
My whole heart is in my throat...
Can't begin to tell you how...
Knowing you're in surgery...
And in a little while...
You will feel pretty lousy...
I can't wait to see you smile...
Just a few more days and then...
You'll exchange your wedding rings...
Les and you will, give a toast...
To "FOREVER" and all it brings...
When I think of my "little girl"...
And all that we've gone through...
You're still my little "softie"...
And I always will love you...
We have had our ups and downs...
Like moms and daughters do...
But no one could be prouder...
Of their daughter...meaning you...
All of us have prayed today...
For things to go just right....
Soon your "owie" will be healed...
And you'll begin to see some "light"...
Then you can just concentrate...
On the life ahead for you....
You and Les and all your kids...
So much love for each other too...!
Always remember, Cari,
Your mommy loves you so...
And I will really miss you all...
When you pack up and have to go...

I LOVE YOU... Mom xoxox...2005

DONNY LOVES MELISSA...

Every parent dreams about... Their child falling in love...
Every parent hopes the girl... Will be sent from heaven above...
The first night at Café Plaka... Love was in your eyes...
Donny's smile was brighter... Than the sunlight in the skies...

Neither of you knew it yet... But you captured each other's hearts...
And from that day and ever more...Of "each other" you'd be a part...
Your tenderness was showing... Her feminine, gentle ways...
Made us hope with all our hearts... She'd be filling Donny's days...

You met when just in high school... You both had separate friends...
Then long distance took you bath apart... And off to different ends...
But the Lord had other plans for you... And went out of his way to show...
That time and distance matters not... When you're in God's path... you know...

He cemented you in His Kingdom... He's guided you both in His care...
He gave you the drive, for His Divine Love... He even gave you His armor to wear...
And all of this time, He was guiding our son... And getting him ready for you...
Instructing him and teaching him ways... To praise "Him" in all he would do...

And through all this time... you still weren't aware... The love that Our Savior imparts...
Was truly the love that you felt in your souls... That He
weaved... "both together"... YOUR HEARTS...
Some of the fears that you both felt... Came crashing all in... all about...
"Forgetting" the Lord made it happen... And casting a shadow of doubt...

But He has His way, and with all of our prayers... He eased all the fears and strife...
He whispered...."Melissa and Donny"... And bonded your two hearts for life...
So Melissa went to Russia... While Donny stayed at home...
Both of you were separate... But your prayers made you never alone...

You're the one we hoped and prayed for... To be our son's dear wife...
To love each other forever... To grow old and spend your life...
A whole world of love is awaiting... Two families to gain, with friends too...
You both get new sisters and brothers... Grandparents, cousins, nephews...

Any tears that we shed are happy ones... We will always be so proud of you...
Though you both leave for Russia...In just a few
weeks... "Together"...you will not be blue...
So, here's to you both...Donny and Mel... May your
love grow much stronger each day...
Forgive and have patience... in all that you do...
Show tenderness in al that you say...
Today as you said your wedding vows... To honor and to love for all time...
Your excitement and joy, could ONLY be matched...
By the joy of DADDY'S AND MINE...
God Bless You on your Wedding Day... And for the rest of your lives...
Written by "Mommy" Margaret Bergeron...January 20, 1996

KERRA MARIN BERGERON...

Born March 18 1997

Have you ever wondered why...God gave you a little girl...?
Ever wonder what He planned...? As you think of her in this world...?

Was it to dress her up real cute...? With all the lace and bows...?
Watching as she twirls around...And does "Tippies" on her toes...

Was it planned for grooming...And teaching her to be...
A young lady, while being strong...Around people she will see...?

Caring for her brother...To honor her Mother and Dad...
Be respectful of all family...And, okay to cry if she's sad...

Teach the principles of life to her...? Show her how to pray...
Let her know she must remember...To do this everyday...!

Wonder if you'll ever stop...Worrying for your "Little Miss"...
Watching as she grows right up...As you get a "Butterfly Kiss"...

So, you thank the Lord for all...The wonders and the worry...
Let her stay a "Little Girl" long...After all, what is the hurry...?

While she says her prayers at night...Feeling love inside your heart...
Being her Mommy and Daddy...Brings joy and love...From the start...

Written by Grammie Margaret
March 1997

MATTHEW GEOFFREY BERGERON...

Born February 25 1999

Did you ever wonder why...God gave you a little boy...?
Ever wonder what He planned...When creating this tiny joy...?

Was it only for your pride...To carry on your name...?
To share the sports and manly things...
So, Dad and Son could "be the same"...

Was it planned for teaching...Your son to be prepared...?
For all the things life brings him...When you hope he isn't scared...?

To show him how to love his Mom...Give examples to his Sis...
How to treat his family someday...Or guide him when life goes "amiss"...

Give the principles of life to him...? Teach him how to pray...?
To lavish him with spiritual gifts...? Even as you play...?

To let him know, right from the start...His goal in life is grand...?
To show responsibility...While taking a firm stand...?

Should you also show him...How much you love his Mom...?
How to cherish and forgive...? Just as you do, Dear son...

So, look upon your little Son...So precious and so new...
He's pleasing to your family...No wonder God gave him to you...

Written By Mommie and Grammie Margaret
February 1999

KAELA JOY BERGERON...

Born August 10, 2001

I was watching you in your bassinette…I knew you couldn't see…
I was wondering, though, if you could feel…How much you mean to me…

Such a tiny miracle…God knew just what to do…
He gave you loving parents…To make, and nourish you…

And your "Big" sister, Kerra…Could hardly wait to touch…
The perfect little bundle…She already loves so much…

You have a "Big" brother too…And, before you were even out…
He talked to his "Baby Kaela"…That's all he talked about…

We knew you were a little girl…Before you were even born…
Buying you pink things and clothes…Just waiting to be worn…

No one, but God, knew just how…Much happiness you'd bring…
Putting so much joy in life…While changing everything…!

Another child to cuddle…Another cherished part…
Completing your little family…With God at the very heart…

Much knowledge you will teach her…While giving her your all…
Growing while she's learning…Before she even learns to crawl…

Another child to grow up strong…Another love to grow…
A wonderful family you have, Dear Ones…
More than you could ever know…

Written by Grammie Margaret
August 10, 2001

EVERYONE SHOULD HAVE AN UNCLE GEORGE...

Everyone should have one...No one should go without...
Ours is extra special... To that...there Is no doubt...

Always makes each day a treat...For everyone you touch...
With your scissors, string and paper... Making trinkets, kites and such...

Every time we look at gifts...You've made that we sure treasure...
Makes us smile and remember...Your life is without measure...

People love you everywhere....Kids love to see your Crafts...
What will Uncle George make next...?
Where you are children will laugh...!

All these years we have been blessed...To have an Uncle George like YOU...
We just want to say "Thanks so much"...For everything you do...

Everyone should have an Uncle George...To make their life complete...
When we get together at holidays it's...
"Uncle George's crafts" and THEN we eat...!

Your efforts and your great ideas...God Is your main concern...
You make "All of us" so happy... No matter where you turn...

After pizza and Birthday cake. ..We'll still be "oh, so blessed"
Cause "everyone should have an Uncle George"...
But, we're lucky..."We have the Best"...!!!

So, what we're really saying is...You are loved and lots of fun...
Everyone should have an Uncle George...
And we have the BEST ONE...

Written by your niece- Margaret Bergeron
May2006

TOM "___" YEARS OLD...

I know that I can't say it loud...Or tell a single soul...
But oh, my special "TOM-PISS"..."You now are -- years old..."
I'll always be your younger sis...Even though you say I'm not...
But, Tom you look so good right now...What it takes, you've got...!
Time has never changed your smile...Your waistline, heart or eyes...
Time has made you all "grown-up"...And also very wise...
It takes a while to build your life...To make a good marriage too...
And many years to grow your kids...And get them both through school...
It takes some years to learn about...Just what God has in store...
And what you have to look forward to...When He blesses you with more...
You've been married many years...With two fantastic sons...
So what if you're getting older...Just think of all the fun...!
Just look around this room right now...And tell us, what do you see...?
A lot of "LOVE" together for you...And this silly poem from me
I've called you "Tom-piss" for many years..."Bag-rats" is my name from you...
I'm only four years behind in age...And you don't see me "BOO-HOO...!
So, once and for all...Who cares about age...?You're only 1 day older...
So what if you're "Half a century" in age...
And your feet keep getting colder...!
Who cares if your hair is thinning...You get tired and fall asleep...
And at night your hands are tingly...And your memory doesn't keep...
Some of us, are right behind...Still some, are way ahead...
As long as we're together right now...Tomorrow, you can stay in bed...!
I kind of thought you'd walk right out...Spend the night right in your car...
And never come back to your party...Or hide out late in the bar...
So, hopefully, (as I write this poem)...I'm reading it right to you...
'Cause there's no where that I'd rather be...Your friends and family too...
So Happy Birthday "DEAR, SWEET TOM"..This day is a special one...
Remembering all the memories...Never forgetting the fun...!

I Love You my special Brother "TOM-PISS"...
YOUR SISTER, "BAG-RATS"
Written by Margaret Bergeron...1994

JAN...

Are you a whole year older...?
Or only just a day...?
Do you feel you're getting better....?
Or does it only look that way...?

Waking up early on Your day...
You really don't know why...
Something about your "birth" day...
Still makes you want to sigh...

Weather won't change your birthday...
Won't change the year gone by...
So, while you can, enjoy yourself...
Make memories, do not cry...

Today's the day that you were born...
And that is quite a thought...
Many people celebrate 'you"...
So, your "birth" day means a lot...

Just a note to let you know...
We care much about your day...
Just look around at your family...
And the love we are sending your way...

So go directly to a mirror..
And smile at who you see...
You are God's special creation...
That's the best that you can be...

Written by Margaret
For Jan, our special sister-in-law
for your Birthday April 2. 1998

LITTLE SOFTIE...

Forty one years ago today... You came into our world...
The apple of your Daddy's eye...And Mommies little girl...

You had a grin from ear to ear...And dimples on your cheeks...
No one could be happier...We were on cloud nine for weeks...

We lived some years in Germany...You were almost three...
Loving cold, the snow and rain...That's where you liked to be...

Such a loving little girl...Little Softie...Cari Buns...
Everyone so in love with you...We were the lucky ones...

You have the softest, smoothest nose...Of anyone I've seen...
And your green eyes dazzle those...Your personality's keen...

You've grown up in all these years...You're a caring, loving Mom...
A great wife to your dear Les... I'm so proud to be your Mom...

I'm writing you this poem today, With a heart that's oh, so sore...
But we just wanted to let you know...We love you to the core...

You gave us all... quite a scare...By being oh, so sick...
Now that we're here, we hope you will.... Recover really quick...

Happy Birthday Cari Lynne..."Softie", you'll always be...
We always miss you on Your day... So here we are, you see!!

Written by your Mommy
Margaret Bergeron
May 5, 2009

BILLY, THE DAY THAT YOU WERE BORN...

Born March 23.1989

The angels must have smiled a lot...On the day that You were born...
Knowing well that you were loved...On that early, warm spring morn...
No one knew how very much...You'd matter to us all...
Seeing you grow up and be...So handsome, smart and tall...
You were our first dear grandchild...And we will not forget...
The joy and fun you've brought to us...Do you melt our hearts...? You bet!
For our Grandchildren are so dear...You make our hearts just burst...
But Billy, you fill a special place.. Because you were the first...
Now, don't you let your head swell UP...Or think you are the best...
You were the first to "get" our love...You got it first, before the rest...!
Though we now can share our love...To more children, as we live...
It means we love you even more...And we have more love to give...!
So Happy 16th BIRTHDAY...you've grown to make us proud...
You make our hearts swell up with love...That we want to shout out loud...
Your life is all laid out for you...So many decisions waiting...
Police Force, or Professional Man.. And also a "little" dating...
You're at a crossroads, YOU can choose...From anything on your plate...
God will help you make the choice...The outcome will be great...!
Billy, you are such a gem...To all that love you so...
Don't be afraid to do "what's right"...SOMETIMES, you must say "NO"...
Take care of Body, Mind, and Soul...Don't EVER forget to PRAY...
For everyone and everything...That you will do each day...
Someday you will look back at this...And remember me and smile...
My words can't even express the love...**THAT**
would take a long, long while...!

Written by Grandma Margaret
March 2005

NICHOLAS

Seems like only weeks ago...
We held you the first time...
A shining star in your Mama's life...
A prize to Grandpa and mine...

We call you Nicky or Doodle Bug...
Pretty soon only "Nick" will do...
Cause you've grown up so fast that, soon...
No one will recognize you...!

The whole world is just in front of you...
The start of your future is now...
The road that you choose is waiting...
It's all up to you...on just how...

You have the very best home life...
Smart, with good grades and great smile...
So loved and so cared about also...
With all this you can go a long while...!

So, Nick, we want you to know that...
You shine and are special and dear...
Cause Grandma and Grandpa can see more...
As we watch you grow older each year...

We love you...
Grandma and Grandpa
December 2001

HAPPY BIRTHDAY TO MY DAD...

Dad, you're really "One of a Kind"...
There's no one else like you...
Loving and understanding me...
Is no easy job to do...

Gosh, Dad, after so many years...
What can I begin to say...?
How do I ever thank you...?
There is no adequate way...

You have given me "life-lessons"...
I never will forget...
You've taught me moral values...
That I cling to...even yet...

Great is not enough for sure...
Describing a Dad like you...
Giving and loving only come close...
"Perfect"...THAT DESCRIBES YOU!!!

So, Daddy, this little message...
Is only a tiny part...
Of all the wonderful memories...
I hold within my heart...

A special occasion seems to be...
Another good time to say...
How very much, that you are loved...
And to wish you a "Happy Birthday"...

Written with love, by your daughter. Margaret -
March 14, 1997

ADELINE...

Sometimes I feel I knew you…
Though, I never saw your face…
They say some things we did alike…
There could be just a trace….

I think of you so many times…
I wish I could have heard…
The way you sang with Julie and Mom…
Like harmony from a bird…

After many years of writing…
And then to find your poems…
It made goose flesh all over…
Like you were visiting my home…

Written by Margaret Bergeron
September 1983   After discovering her poem book…

MICHAEL D. SCHADE...

How many years have we all been friends...?Since 1967...
Sharing our lives in West Berlin...Was a little slice of Heaven...!

It could have been a lonely place...But we really had a ball...
Especially when our apartment, was...Next to yours, right down the hall...

Being in the Air Force...Patrolling around the town...
You puking in the air...Boxers flying, flagpole bound...

Cooking and eating were pastimes ...All the gang was together...
We had fun drinking and munching...No matter how awful the weather...

Learning about all our families...Where we all lived our lives...
Seeing our babies quickly grow up...Friends,
children, husbands and wives...

Not many know of the bonding...That takes place, so far away...
So glad we stayed friends all these years, Mike...
And that's what this poem will say...

Thanks for all the fun visits...For calling us every New Years...
For making us know that you love us...For
listening, when we were in tears...

You've been through our life, right here with us...
Seen us through thick and through thin...
Just looking back at the pictures...Shows just
what great friends we have been...

So this is just our little present...You know, you are one special friend...
The kind that will travel our lifetime...And last
after most friendships must end...

Written By Margaret Bergeron
Edited By Bill Bergeron
2000

MARILYN LOVES JIM...

How do you begin to write...
About a pair like you...
Our friendship started long ago...
And we'll always be joined to you…

Jim, we've known you "30" years...
Marilyn, over "20"...
Thru "ins" and "out's" of all our lives...
We have all shared plenty...

Your vows are very sacred words...
To promise your all and more...
Asking your children, family and friends...
As witnesses…forevermore...

"Been there" from DAY ONE for you...
We're "Friends for Life" agree...?
Growing old together...
That's how friendship ought to be...

On this Special Occasion…
We ask Our Lord to bless...
Your day today and all your life...
With perfect happiness...
We Love you…

Margaret and Bill
April 26, 1997

THE KITCHENAIRES...

Honoring our Mother...
Has surely made her day...
Knowing how she loves you all...
Here's what she'd probably say

"Oh, you shouldn't be so nice..."
"I don't deserve it all"...
"Someone else is better"...
"For a party at the hall"...

"I can't believe how nice you are...
"To someone such as me"...
"I only play the piano"...
'How hard can that be"...?

Every week on Wednesdays...
She packs her "music purse"...
Choosing just the right songs...
For you to all rehearse...

The Band means so **very** much to Mom...
She's always concerned about...
Never wanting to conflict...
Or leaving anyone out...

Music, friends and laughter...
Her smile, her love and glow...
You all mean so much to her...
And she'd want you all to know...

Thank you for all the love and care...
That you give to Mom each day...
I'm so glad you're **all** her Friends...
And that's what I wanted to say...!

Written by Margaret Bergeron
2006

204

CHRIS... "DOCTOR HAL"...

Some people call you Dr. Chris...
Dr. Hal by others too...
You'll answer to Halamandaris...
Or "Hal" is fine with you...

You mostly always have a smile…
Sometimes a questioned brow....
You seem to care for everyone...
We just can't figure how...

Your hands are trained to move our bones…
Your diagnosis is to care…
Your mind's conditioned to feel our pain…
And knowledge you always share…

You anticipate appointments…
(Lose sleep when you have to write...)
Your staff reflects your loving ways…
You've been their guiding light…

You help your patients feel their best…
You know you've been a part…
Of all the happy backs and necks…
God blessed your hands (and heart)…

How do we say how much we care...?
When thank-you just won't do....?
We find someone to write a poem…
ESPECIALLY FOR YOU…

Written by Margaret Bergeron
April 1998

205

MICHAEL LOVES KIM...

Love surely is a funny thing...
It follows wherever you go...
No matter how often you've been apart...
Your "love" just seems to grow...

Love glows when you say "you're sorry"...
Be sure and give good hugs...
Consider each other in all that you do...
Don't sweep feelings under the rug...

Remember all the fun things you do...
Continue to laugh and tease...
If you can keep the courtship alive...
Your relationship will "bloom" with ease...

That means to open up your heart...
To love, to trust, to give...
Your love can endure everything...
As long as you may live...

We Love You Lots....

Margaret and Bill
August 15, 1997

DONNY …

Another Birthday milestone…We've had you near our side…
Going through life's phases…At times, just along for the ride…

So many changes have taken place…Since we worried hand in hand…
Wondering where you'd wander…Playing castles in the sand…

So much was going on in that…Little head up there…
So mixed up and so confused…In that sad and lonely stare…

I've prayed so hard to God each day…Lord, take him in your care…
Make him grow up happy…Let him know how much "we" care…

The days and years took longer…We feared we could not cope…
Just when everything else had failed…God gave us some more hope…

Back then, it seemed so hard to do…To follow all the rules…
Counseling, teachers, doctors…Constant turmoil in the schools…

And now you have a family…Why did we have such fears…?
God did answer all our prayers…It just took a few more years…

Kerra, Matthew, Kaela…With Melissa as your bride…
Such a gorgeous family…Standing side by side…

We are so proud of everything…You bring to all our lives…
God holds you tightly with HIS hand…Your children and your wife…

Happy Birthday Donny…How blessed we are to see…
Just how far that you have come…And completed our family…

We love you so much…Sorry about all the fuss…
No real words could ever express…How much you mean to us…

Written by Your Mommy
September 21, 2009

JUDY AND PATTY...

You've given yourselves unselfishly...
Without a second thought...

Two real live "Florence Nightingales"...
With all the love you've brought...

You've no idea how much it helped...
My Momma and for me...

You're what Our God had ordered...
What we're all supposed to be...

The tender strength of just your hugs...
Your presence, smiles and care...

I could take a break with confidence...
Just knowing you were there...

When I think back to all the days...
That I have called on you...

It reminds me of God smiling...
Giving friendships to pull me through...

So even if I've said it...
A million times before...

Thank you and God bless you...
For your friendships, and much more...

Written by Margaret Bergeron
February 2005

OUR MOM...

Oh, the years that you have loved us...And attended to us all...
You always had room, (and food for more)...
No matter who would call...Whenever I think of Mother's Day...
(Although, I am one too)...I only think of you today...
There is no MOM like you...
You taught us generosity...You're giving to a fault...
If someone stole your pepper...You'd offer them your salt...!
You showed us about caring...Comforting family and friends...
How to open up our hearts...Your teaching never ends...
You gave us opportunities...To reach, to grow and learn...
You allowed us to stumble, sometimes to fall...
But you were there at every turn...
You fed us, (as only you knew how)...Enough for the whole block....
Not only three full meals a day...But food around the clock...!
You listened with understanding,...And that's no easy task...
Whether you wanted to hear it or not...Did we ever EVEN bother to ask...?
You looked upon us with worry...How could you help but see...
The many mistakes that we would make...
Formed the people we would be...
Capturing the hearts of family and friends...
Your Grandchildren, big and small...
You have so much love in your heart for Dad...
That it overflows enough for us all...
Mother's Day was made for you...My Mother, my helper, my friend...
Saying "thank-you" is not enough...So this message I will send...
You've comforted, taught and fed us...Attended, cared and given...
Been generous, worried and prayed for years...
And responsible for our living...
You've done everything humanly possible...To give us, all that you do...
The biggest and best thing, though, is your love...
And ours, is what We Send to you...!

With so much love, always...
Margaret and Bill
Written by Margaret Bergeron...1998

OUR DAD...

Dad, you've been the best there is…
That's how we must begin…

From the kindness of your gentle heart…
To the cleft in your dear chin…

Dad, in all your "90" years…
You've surely paid your dues…

Mom even told us that "no one"…
Could ever fill your shoes…

So here's to the man we love so-o much…
For all the love you've shown…

For all the sacrifices you've made…
Just trying to get us grown…

We love you… Happy Birthday Dad…
All of your children, grandchildren,
Great-grandchildren and all that love you so much…

Written by your daughter, Margaret
Margaret Bergeron…March 14, 2008

GRANDBABIES...

Few things in life...
Could ever compare...
To the birth of a baby...
So tiny, so fair..

What a miracle, really...
God grants us each day...
He fashioned our bodies...
In such unique ways...

The birth of our grandchild...
Just happened today...
We stood there in awe...
No words could we say...

Two grandmas together...
Holding each other tight...
Watching as our children...
Turned into parents...overnight...

Her first breath in this great world...
Caused the ground to shake...
Then we realized that it was...
A 5.5 earthquake...

If that is an indication...
Of statements she will make...
This "Baby Girl" is going to soar...
And no guff...will she take...

So now our joys and attentions...
Are wrapped in pink bows and lace...
God's creation was, born tonight...
An angel...with soft cherub face...

Written for Kerra Marin Bergeron by her
Grandma. Margaret Bergeron,
March 18, 1997

JAYNE

We were neighbors for a reason... More than forty years ago...
Do things happen, just by chance...?No, I don't think so...

How our lives would all be changed... If, we did not know you...
How we'd miss the friendship... And your cute accent too...

You are the kind of friend, (to me)... That really melts my heart...
All those years on Paraiso Way... You were such an important part...

I babysat your children... When I was only ten...
Mee-Maw kept a watchful eye... 'Til you came home again...

I did your hair for twenty years...Cut and color too...
You're already beautiful... What wrong could I do...?

Years have passed, time has too... But some things stay the same...
You still make me smile real big... Whenever I hear your name...

We celebrate your Birthday... Eighty years of life...
Four great children, grandkids... And, you were an A-I wife...

Jayne, you always listened... We never had to hide...
Doing hair at Dorothy's house... We all smoked and laughed and cried...

We have so many memories... Seems like only yesterday...
Time may pass, but not the love... It's still the same today...

HAPPY BIRTHDAY JAYNE
We Love you, Margaret and Bill
July 7, 2000

LES IS " 58 " NOW...

We know that we can say it loud...And tell a hundred souls...
You are a special "Son-in-law"...And you're "58" years old...!
We'll always be your in-laws...And we'll put you on the spot...
For "58" you look pretty good...What it takes, you got...!

Time could never change your smile...Your caring heart, or eyes...
Time has made you all grown up...And also, very wise...!
It takes a while to build your life...To make a good marriage too...!
And many years to grow your kids...And get them all through school...

It takes some time to learn about...Just what God has in store...
Think of all the fun ahead...When He blesses you some more...!
Cari loves you, oh, so much...The kids know you're the best...!
So what if you're getting older...You've conquered all the rest...!

Just look around the room right now...What do you see...?
A LOT OF "LOVE" together for you...And, this silly poem from me...!
So, once and for all...who cares about age...?..You're only one day older...
So what, if it's (more than) "HALF A CENTURY"...
And your feet keep getting colder..

Who cares if your hair starts thinning...? You get tired and fall asleep...
And at night your hands get tingly...And your memory doesn't keep...
Some are right behind you... (Some of us are way ahead)...
As long as we're together...Tomorrow, you can stay in bed...

You really are a special guy...How could we ever repay...?
For making our family happy...In every single way...
I wish that we were there right now...Reading this right to you...
'Cause, there's nowhere we would rather be...
With your friends, and us (and you...!)

SO, HAPPY "58th" BIRTHDAY LES...THIS IS A SPECIAL ONE...
REMEMBER ALL THE MEMORIES...
NEVER FORGET THE FUN...!

WE LOVE YOU,
Margaret and Bill
July 25, 2009

MELISSA'S LABOR CANDLE...

This is Melissa's Labor Candle...
Light it on that day...

Reminding you to say a prayer...
For when, Kaela comes out to stay...

It also will remind you...
To keep them in your thoughts...

While she is pushing Kaela out...
Hoping, it won't hurt a lot...

Light the other one for Donny...
Pray for him won't you...?

Being a daddy for Number three...
Kaela, Kerra, and Matthew too...!

And when the waiting is over...
When Mel's labor is all done...

They'll know that they were prayed for...
By every single one...

Written by Grammie Margaret
June 25, 2001

F. F. B. W. H. A. B.
WHERE DO WE BEGIN...

TOR AND FAL AND BRES, YOU ARE...THE
FRIENDS I'LL ALWAYS TREASURE...
THE LOVE I FEEL FOR YOU INSIDE...
COULD NEVER HAVE A MEASURE...

THANKS FOR CONSIDERATION...FOR THE
GENTLENESS YOU'VE SHOWN...
YOUR FRIENDSHIP GOES WAY, WAY ABOVE...
OF OTHER FRIENDS I'VE KNOWN...

SO MANY YEARS HAVE COME AND GONE...
AND, STILL, YES...HERE WE ARE...
WE'LL ALWAYS HAVE CONNECTIONS...
NO MATTER, NEAR OR FAR...

OUR LIVES ARE ALL SO DIFFERENT...BUT,
AS FRIENDS, REMAINS THE SAME...
OUR FAMILIES, SO IMPORTANT...WE
KNOW THEM ALL BY NAME...

WE LAUGH & TALK & EAT & DRINK...
AND LAUGH & TALK SOME MORE...
THE MINUTE THAT WE SEE EACH OTHER...
'TIL WE SAY "BYE" AT THE DOOR...

THROUGH SCHOOL AND COLLEGE, KIDS AND
SUCH...MOVING, SICKNESS, HEALTH...
FIRES, DEATH AND GRANDKIDS...WHETHER
POOR, OR BLESSED WITH WEALTH...

TORREY, YOU LIKE CHARDONNAY...
BRES "CHAMPAGNE'S THE BEST"...
FAL LIKES EITHER ONE, OR BOTH...I LIKE
TEQUILA FROM THE REST...!

ONE OF US IS EARTHY...ONE (OR MORE)
CAN'T HEAR TOO WELL...

WE ALL ARE DIFFERENT, BUT THE SAME...
AND FOR US, THAT WORKS OUT SWELL...

THE TIME IS SHORT FOR OUR GETAWAY...
BUT, WE SURE CRAMMED IN A LOT...
SOME THINGS WE'LL CARRY IN OUR HEARTS...
AND GIVE US LOTS OF THOUGHT...

SOME THINGS MAKE US LAUGH OUT LOUD...
LIKE "GARDENING AND VEET"...
SNORING ALL IN UNISON...LITTLE
TOES ON SHEELAGH'S FEET...
PHONE CALLS, JUST FOR "CHECKING IN"...
FROM THOSE WE LOVE AT HOME...
KNOWING THAT WE'RE MISSED A LOT...WHEN
WE CAN FIGURE OUT OUR PHONES...!

SO, AS WE WIND OUR PARTY DOWN...
AS WE HAVE THIS NEXT GOOD-BYE...
TONIGHT WE'LL CELEBRATE OUR BONDS...
EVEN IF IT MAKES US CRY...
WE CAN BE OURSELVES TOGETHER...BE
SAD, TELL THE TRUTH, OR CRUDE...?
BUT DEEP INSIDE, OUR LOVE STILL SHOWS...
OUR LOVE IS NEVER RUDE...

SO, DEAR FRIENDS, THIS POEM'S FOR YOU...
WRITTEN WITH SO MUCH CARE...
THANK YOU FOR ALL THE FUN WE'VE HAD...
AND FOR ALWAYS BEING THESE...
SO, WITH THAT <u>WE HAVE BEGUN</u> !!!
I LOVE YOU ALL, MAG-RET...JULY 2007...FRIENDS
FOREVER BECAUSE WE HAVE A BOND
F.F.B.W.H.A.B.

Written to me by our daughter!!!

HAPPY 60th MOMMY...

Today you turn 60...
It doesn't seem true to me...
You still look only 40...
Oh how did you... How could it be....?

A mother we can cherish...
And be so proud of...
You have shown us all...
The true meaning of love...

Just a phone call away...
You are always there to listen...
Or just to blow off steam...
There does not have to be a reason...

I have relied on you, all of my life...
You have never let me down...
You even took a plane ...
All the way to my little town...

You took such good care of me...
I'm sorry for the scare (or two)...
I am just so lucky to know...
You are always there (Yahoo)...

So happy Birthday Mom...
You're the greatest, what a pearl...
My love for you is endless...
Love your little girl...

March 20 2007
Written with love by Cari Ablondi
Little Softie

FATHER'S DAY...

Dads... they are the best there is...
That's how we must begin...
From the kindness of their gentle hearts...
To the cleft in their dear chin...

Dads... in all their many years...
Have surely paid their dues...
Moms have even told us that...
No one could fill their shoes...

Here's to the men, we love so-o-o much...
For all the love they've shown...
For all the sacrifice they made...
Just trying to "get us grown"...

For all the times they were right there...
To soothe those growing fears...
Even though we're grown up now...
We still recall those years...

So thanks to all the Fathers...
Husbands, Uncles, Grandpas too...
Life would be a lonesome place...
Without the love from you...

Written by Margaret Bergeron
June 2002

THE BIRKENSTOCK...

Once, upon a time...
Not too long ago...
Josh and Andrew used their mouths...
Talked back, when JIM said, "NO!"...
Bickering and crying...
In a very tiny car...
With Big Bill and Big Dad Jim...
While traveling very far...

It was hot, the car was too...
Across the Texas Plains...
100 + and tempers flared...
Bill couldn't pull back his reins...
The first thing he could think of...
Before he lost his cool...
Was to throw his "Size 12" Birkenstock...
(A very handy tool...)
They also did their "Sassy Dance"...
The LAST TIME behind his back...
'Cause Big Bill saw their tongues come out...
And threw those shoes with a WACK...
It sure got their attention...
And as far as we all know...
Was the last time they talked back to Jim...
And to Bill, they NEVER said NO...

So now you know why BIG BILL'S SHOES...
Are stored inside their box...
They'll never be able to FLY AGAIN...
BUT, BOY, THEY DO STILL TALK...!!!

Written by Margaret Bergeron...With help from BIG BILL...2007

YOGI...

Yogi was my bestest friend...
Always there for me...
Content to wait throughout the day...
Knowing faithfully where I'd be...

Surfing at our favorite beach...
He knew it made me glad...
Having my best "Pal" in my truck...
Best feeling I ever had...

And through the years his eyes grew dim...
Those big ears muffled a bit...
He knew my voice and gentle hug...
But it hurt him a little to sit...

He just laid down and waited...
He didn't ask for much...
Listening for me arriving home...
And loving my familiar touch...

You'll always be my "best pal"
No one could take your place...
Whenever I think of a faithful friend...
I'll instantly remember your face...

Written for Dr. Hal...And his dog Yogi
By Margaret Bergeron
September 1997

CAN WE EVER TALK !

It started out quite differently...This friendship with my friend...
We've shared and cried and laughed out loud...Now there will be no end...

Always there for each other...Across the telephone lines...
Talking sometimes for hours...In the best and worst of times...

The things that happen to my friend...Can barely be believed...
When she just makes it home at night...You really feel relieved...

God is working in her life...She's not sure when or how...
"In His Time" takes on a new meaning...
Since she wants her answers now!!!...

The tears we've shed could flood a lake...The laughs could crack your face...
The "Oh, no not again's" could fill...The air in outer space...

We used to smoke 'til late each night...And when she quit, I sighed...
I said, "I'll never be able to stop..."And when I did, she cried...

We can talk about most anything...We laugh hard until we cry...
Working together, we were great pals...Then we had to say good-bye...

No matter where you go, my friend...You'll never get rid of me...
And even 'til the day we die...Sisters, we'll always be...

'Cause God has had His hand on us...And He promised us his Grace...
So even in Heaven, we'll be friends...I'll still smile upon your face...

And, by the way, in Heaven...There are no tears to shed...
So we will have to sing and play...And be happy and glad instead...

To my friend, Penny.. .with, so much love.

Written by Margaret Bergeron ...
September 1997

GERALD 'JERRY' BLOCK

He is quiet and conservative...
Keeps his thoughts inside his head...
Whistles Christmas tunes all year...
Always thinking...and well-read...
Never heard him laugh out loud...
Does not want a "whole story" told...
Asks how you are, then continues on...
With a new case to unfold...

He is a no nonsense kind of guy...
The kind you are glad to know...
Because if he is your attorney...
The "other side" has got to go...
He is neat, precise and knows his work...
And does not like much change...
The computer, he will tolerate...
But try not to rearrange...

His family is his # 1...
He beams with joy and pride...
He has a family filled with girls...
And Lois, his lovely bride...
Gerald Block...Attorney at Law...
You are quite the all around guy...
You have made a lot of clients smile...
And the opposition sigh......

And as a boss, you truly are...
The nicest there could be...
That is why I had to write this poem...
Though you probably will not agree...
So, here is to you Jerry, just because...
Sometimes it is nice to hear...
That a lot of people appreciate you...
Each day...throughout the year...

Written by Margaret Bergeron
March 1998

DONNA...

This poem is just for Donna...
(Sometimes we call her Tor!) ...
Friends like her are seldom found...
That is what I am writing for...

We have been friends 40 years (at least)...
And not one year has passed...
Without keeping together...
Our friendship was built to last...

This poem is only touching some...
Of what we want to say...
So much has happened in all those years...
Leading clear up to today...

However, if we named them all...
My pen would lose its ink...
My hand would be all cramped up...
My poor eyes would not blink...

So just a word of thanks for all...
The kind things that you have done...
For caring so much and showing love...
And for sharing a whole day of fun...

We truly love you...
Margaret and Bill
October 1997

SUE ...

How do I write a poem for Sue...?
How do I dare begin...?
Should I start with 50's...
And the mischief we got in...?
Should I talk about our blue shorts...
Scarves, sweaters and Vaseline...?
Mother Gemma getting mad at us...?
'Til she probably wanted to scream...

Laughing hard during confession time...
Getting giggles during mass...
Wondering if our bra marks showed...
Before we went to class...
And the carnivals were so much fun...
We thought we were so cool...
Curled our lashes and shined our lips...
Got in trouble when we got to school...

Let the boys walk us home from school...
Took vacations, we were never apart...
Trying so hard to be grown up...
We each held the other's heart...
We drifted away for quite a while...
A lot happened in between...
Shed some tears and lost some years...
Since we were only teens...

But here we are all grown up now...
With stories, and some pains...
God has been with us for sure...
To get us through those rains...
Now it is your Birthday...
So Happy Birthday Sue...
May you be blessed with everything...
That makes life the best for you...!

Written especially for Sue Peters by Margaret
June 22, 2005

(Written for Tom and Jan)

TRACY MY "NEW-FOUND" LITTLE GIRL...

Every day I thought: about...(and oh. your mom did too)...
Wondered what your life was like...We prayed that they loved you...
Each year, on your birthday...Not one year would go by...
Without our thoughts focused on you...It always made us cry...
I wondered if you looked like your mom...Did you think of us some days...?
Having great brothers like Ryan and Chad...
What words would you and I say...?
So many times I pictured you...And all that time we missed...
All the hugs and memories...Will start with days like this...

The day our prayers were finally heard...God's answer was plain to see...
Our little girl named Tracy...Was revealed to your Mom and me...
Your life was good and you were loved...By friends and family...
Your Mom prayed so hard everyday...So that one day you would see...
That someone else did love you so...Thought of you in every way...
Your parents took good care of you...So, we
would meet them too someday...
You have a family of your own...Six children in your care...
And such a loving husband...What joys we get to share...!

And so, the time has come at last...We finally get to meet...
The daughter we have dearly missed...To make our lives complete...!
Tracy, we're so proud of you...With all that you have done...
Showing so much compassion...Loving your daughters and sons...
The kindness you are showing to others...Shows your "heart" in all you do...
God blessed you with two loving families...
And we feel more blessed having you...
Your love in return is our bonus...A Daughter, Grandchildren, and Sons...
In turn you have gained a huge family...Who welcome you our special one...!

This joy will keep getting stronger...Can't contain it, not one second more...
Until we finally can see you...In front of us, right at the door...!
Today is a day I remember...As long as I live I will say...
"Moms face lights up when she hears you"...
Please know that I feel the same way...

Dictated with love, by your "New found" DAD

Composed and written by your Auntie Margaret
May 2004

GOD, PLEASE USE ME

All she wanted to do is surf...
And have a little fun...
She was the best at what she did...
And was loved by everyone...
Her life was great...so young and still...
So much to see and do...
Then, just as fast...everything changed...
God was holding Bethany too...
A big shark dared to end my life...
And Satan thought he would drop by...
Filling my heart with doubt and fear...
Until God said, "Nice Try!"...

Then I knew God was using me...
To show it can be done...
Use my pain and character...
Reaching out to everyone...

Paddling with one arm is tough...
But, surfing, I can do...
Proving anything in life can start...
With God...in your life too...

Almost, unbelievable...
The day her world stood still...
Yet she said, "God, Please Use Me!"...
"I am still alive" "and its YOUR Will"...

"Dear God, please use me in this life"...
"To tell how wonderful, how true"...
"So that everyone will see"...
"That none could love like YOU"...

Here I am, my life is proof...
That God can use you too...
All you do, is pray and ask...
That is all you have to do...

Written by Margaret Bergeron...2008
For Bethany Hamilton

LOIS...

GOD KNEW...

God knew I had to live near you...
So He put me right next door...
Then He gave us Splash class...
So we'd be friends "for shore!"

Then He gave compassion...
And hearts to open wide...
To help with daily struggles...
And to help us keep in stride...

He tells us to depend on Him...
To give Him all we've got...
That means all our worries...
(Even though we've got a lot!!)

He promised He'd always be right here...
Holding our friendship hearts...
He knows how we need each other...
And we have right from the start...

So, Lois, this poem's for you...
With the love that friendship brings...
You are a true "forever friend"...
You're one of my favorite things...

Happy Birthday Lois...
Written by your "Forever Friend" Margaret
November 17, 2006

A GOOD FRIEND...

Someone who first thinks about...
The needs and cares of you...
Sees to all the details...
Before the day is through...

Never seems to mind too much...
When things don't work out right...
Keeps their wits about them...
Most every day and night...

Makes you feel important...
Listens with deep care...
Truly tries to help you out...
Anytime and anywhere...

Has a calming quality...
Every time they're near...
Friendship is all they want from you...
And sometimes to lend an ear...

Always there in bad times...
And for the good times too...
Showing up with love and words...
Always a friend to you...

If you have a friend like this...
A good person, honest and true...
God has blessed you richly...
By giving this friend to you...

Some have friends that come and go...
Some no friends at all...
Do you have a special friend...?
Sit down and give them a call...!

Written by Margaret Bergeron...1995

JEANNE...

So many years you made me feel... Relaxed, just like a rag...
Made me comfortable, at ease... And now...I get to brag...

Your such a special person...Always soothing all my aches...
Using oil that smells so good... But, your hands are what it takes...

Remembering important things...About my family...
Taking care with feelings...Always listening to me...

I also like to hear about...Your life and what it holds...
Laughing about the silly things... How your new house unfolds...

Letting my mind be at rest...Massaging my sore joints...
Helping my body to get well... Never missing those pressure points...

You are a special friend to me...One I felt so blessed to meet...
Caring for the top of my head... All the way down to my feet...!

God has surely gifted you...Given YOU a generous heart...
Blessed every person you ever touch... Whomever you become a part...

Thank you, Jeanne, for being the friend... That you have come to be...
I hope someday, you will know how much... You have meant to me...

HAPPY BIRTHDAY August 10,2001
Love, Margaret

WANKA...

Wonder how this young girl... Not even "planned" to be...
Stayed alive despite the odds... She claimed her destiny...

She endured such torment... Through rape, abuse and pain...
She still forgave and cared for all... Her hardship was her gain...

Seemed, the worse they treated her... Instilled a stronger will...
Taking care of everyone... And a little girl...still...

Surviving her stepfather's fury... Nursed her mother's sickness too...
Endured her horrid grandmother...But her dream was coming true...

She worked so hard for freedom... And finally, came the day...
She did not know the language... Or a soul in the USA...

But a fighter and determined... Claimed her place and made the best...
Of all that life could offer... And put aside the rest...

Found her way to New York State... Working more than sleep...
Making friends that made her smile... And a way of life to keep...

This book will show forgiveness... Makes you want to hug her heart...
Made her life so full of love... When it could have been torn apart...

For Wanka was not wanted... But "that" was not to be...
Becoming everything "good" instead... A surprise, as you will see...

Makes you think, could this be real...? Was there such a girl as this...?
How could she overcome such strife...? It is a life you will not dismiss...

Written by Margaret A. Bergeron, for Sonita De La Barcas book, "WANKA"
October 2000

GREYHOUNDS...

Their stature is royal...
Lean muscle, and strong...
Though, aerodynamic...
To race them, is wrong...

Behind those big "doe" eyes...
Linger, sweetness and grace...
Under the smooth skin...
And the beautiful face...

Beats a heart like a human...
Dedicated and true...
For the love of their family...
So blessed, if it is you...

The mild mannered Greyhound...
Is so eager to please...
So calm and appealing...
You love them with ease...

They depend on you solely...
No demands, little care...
There is no shedding on carpets...
`Cause they hardly have hair...

Whenever you meet one...
You are hooked from the start...
If you rescued a Greyhound...
You have captured a heart...

Written By Margaret Bergeron
For Jeanne, Wells and Sandee
November 2000

BRIANNA, TIFFANY AND BROOKE...

Miss Mandy knew her trio...
Were not" Just Plain Dancing" girls...
They dance with entertainment...
That can start your head to whirl...

Barely even ten years old...
Still little girls at heart...
Slumber parties, beach and fun...
But dancing was their start...

Friends that play and dance each day...
Brianna, Tiff and Brooke...
Giving joy this afternoon...
As we tap our toes and look...

Thank you girls for treating us...
To an afternoon with you...
You certainly brighten many eyes...
And softened our hearts too...!

Written by Margaret Bergeron
August 2003

MARKUS...

How do we write about Mark...?
And all the traits of you...?
That make our Mark so special...
And a "little" different too...!

It is true, you don't like green things...
Like lettuce or salad stuff...
For sure, no type of "garnish" ...
And "no waiting" ...but that is enough...!

Your friendship has been constant...
Been close for many years...
Ups and downs, sick and well...
Said prayers and shed some tears...

We also shared tequila...
Even shared the same small glass...
Laughed a million times and even...
Showed a little class...

Been through church, babies and kids...
Said goodbye to Marilyn & Jim...
Taco Surf, Birthdays and barbeques...
(We sure owe a lot to them)...

You are the special Birthday Boy...
So we are gathering tonight...
To wish you wealth, happiness and health...
And a Birthday that is just right...

Friends like us are here to stay...
Our lives just intertwine...
When it comes to friendships...
You can count on Bills and mine...

Love and Happy Birthday, Mark

From Margaret and Bill
July 11, 2003

AUNT IRMA...

You always think of others...
Hugging, deep within your heart...
You have the softest, dearest touch...
We knew that from the start...

You always let your kindness show...
With your endearing smile...
We have never seen you angry...
Just a tear, (once in a while)...

Today, it is your Birthday...
And you are such a "Special Aunt"...
This poem sends a hug to you...
Since we are not there, we can't...

So, here is to every happiness...
That you are so deserving of...
Between the lines of this poem...
Is stuffed with lots of love...

Happy Birthday, Aunt Irma...
Love, Margaret and Bill

Written by Margaret
October 1999

AUNT JULIE AND UNCLE LOU...

I have some special relatives.. In Reno, they reside...
They BELONG in California... 'Cause Nevada is a long ride...

They enjoy life to the fullest... Volunteering, golf and such...
Spoiling their four grandkids... They love them a whole bunch...

Their daughter Kathy, lives in Carson... With
her children and husband Steve ...
Julie could not be prouder...Lou beams, like you would not believe...

They say its "oh, so beautiful"... In their little gamblin' town...
Enjoying every minute... As they drop those nickels down...

They have grown to know celebrities... That entertain each night...
Who know about the "sisters"... Singing songs to them just right...

Opening your home to everyone... That takes the 12 hour drive...
Change the beds, prepare some food... Make the whole house come alive...

The long awaited visit...From Harold and Clarice..
Who come to play and just relax... And they bring Aunt Janece..

Aunt Irma and Aunt Ada too...You must go see them all...
Plan a lunch or outing... You'll surely have a ball...

The plans and dates and dinners... Keep all of you so busy...
The week is gone before you know... And leaves you in a tizzy...

Then time comes to give "those" hugs... The ones that say "good bye"...
Knowing you will be oh, so sad... Just makes you want to cry...

Just so you will not get lonely... As everyone drives away...
You are loved by all of us.. And in our hearts, you will stay...

So plan your meals for next time... Book all the shows and lunches...
Gather all the Grandkids... Tell the family, plan the brunches...

Something to look forward to... Each day you get to smile...
Enjoy the day that God has made... Savor it awhile...!
Written by Margaret Bergeron
October 18, 1999

A GOOD HAPPY BIRTHDAY...

LIVE...
ALLOW YOURSELF TO THINK...
ALWAYS HAVE A SMILE ON YOUR FACE...
ALWAYS TELL YOUR LOVED ONES THAT YOU LOVE THEM.....
LOOK UP OLD FRIENDS...
MAKE A NEW ONE EVERY DAY...
GROW UP A LITTLE EACH DAY...
HOPE FOR THE BEST....
GIVE YOUR ALL...
CHEER THE MOST...
PICK ROSES...
GIVE THEM ALL AWAY...
ALWAYS KEEP YOUR WORD...
LAUGH OUT LOUD...
OPEN UP YOUR HEART...
LET SOMEONE IN...
HUG ALL CHILDREN...
TAKE TIME TO BREATHE...
REALLY GAZE UPON A SUNSET...
LISTEN TO THE THUNDER...
FEEL THE RAIN...
TRUST IN GOD...
HAVE FAITH IN YOUR TRUST...
MAKE SOME MISTAKES...
LEARN FROM THEM...
ENJOY EACH DAY...
WANDER AROUND WITH CAUTION...
ENJOY YOUR SEARCHINGS...
NEVER GIVE UP...
SOMETIMES GIVE IN...
BE AMAZED BY EVERYTHING...
CELEBRATE ALL LIFE...
AND TODAY CELEBRATE YOURS.........

Written by Margaret Bergeron
June 1998.

ON YOUR BIRTHDAY...

Are you a whole year older...?
Or only just a day...?
Do you think you're getting older...?
Or does it only feel that way...?

Waking up early on your day...
You really don't know why...
Getting ready for school today...
You were a cheer-y guy...

The weather won't change your birthday...
Won't change the years gone by...
So, while you can enjoy your day...
Make memories, (some day you will know why)...

Today's the day that you were born...
And that is quite a thought...
Many people celebrate "you"...
So your birthday means a lot...

So go directly to a mirror...
And smile at who you see...
'Cause you are God's creation...
That's the best that you can be...

Written by Grandma Bergeron
For Billy a special Grandson...
March 23, 1998

MOM...I'M ON MY WAY HOME...

Another state does have its charm...The trees and hills and space....
But Arkansas is too far away...And I miss your smiling face...

Child care costs so much these days...You said you missed the boys...
Daddy could take them to the beach...(We wouldn't bring all their toys!)...

Our furniture could all be stored...Until we find a house...
I'd help you clean and cook each day...And be quiet as a mouse...

Maybe you could help me out...Picking up the boys from school...
Helping with their homework...Teaching the golden rule...

Because I can find a job out there...To help in every way...
So you don't worry about anything...Hey, mom, what do you say...?

I'll talk to Daddy if you wish... I <u>know</u> he will agree...
That living together, (just for a while)...Could be fun for the kids and me...

I promise it won't be for too long...I know you need your space...
Because you and Daddy have been alone...
And you don't have a real big place...

But, I'm in need of help right now...I have no where else to turn...
I want the kids around you both...And with your help to learn

That family life is what they need...And truly what we miss...
Saying goodnight is not the same...Without Grandma and Grappa's kiss...

I'm packing all our things right now...Hoping it won't take too long...
Because we love and miss you so...
Close to family...is where we belong...

Written by Mommy in anticipation of Cari, Billy and Nicky's arrival...
1997

EVERYONE HAS A PLACE...

Everyone has a place they hide...
Deep inside our hearts...
A place that only God can fill...
Only He can fill that part...

An empty place that waits for us...
To change our worried ways...
Turn over all the cares and woes...
Surrender all our days...

Give yourselves completely to God...
Every part of you...
For you want to be tools for Him...
In everything you do...

For the eyes of the Lord search the world...
For people's perfect hearts...
So He can show His power...
In helping every part...

If you give up just anything...
For the love of God this day...
He'll give you a hundred times over...
That's a wonderful promise, I'd say...

Written by Margaret Bergeron
June 2003

A MATTER OF CHOICE...

When you wake up each morning...
What's the first thing that you do...?
Do you give your day to God...?
So He can dwell in you...?
Do you pray for all your family...
Your neighbors, friends and foe...
When you're making a decision...
Do you pray, "Which way should I go...?"
Do you look around your life...
Being grateful for all you see...?
Do you share your love and things...?
Or just think of "me, me, me..."
You have much more than many...
And less than many more...
But what you really have my friend...
Is not what lies behind your door...
The trinkets that we accumulate...
Are pleasing to our eyes...
Cars and our possessions...
That all our money buys...
Can't bring our toys with us...
No matter where we look...
All that we will really need...
Is our name in heaven's book...
Our Kingdom is in heaven...
God planned a place for you...
So don't store up too many things...
And that means money too...!
Many choices are before you...
Every single day...
Ask God to guide you through them...
There is no better way...
Choose to love with all your heart...
Let it grow and sprout...
Light loves candle, let it glow...
It never will blow out...

Written by Margaret Bergeron
September 2003

THINGS I KNOW FOR SURE...

That God made this wonderful world...
With all the beauty and space...
He made us all in His image...
Every single different face...

He filled the sky with Sun, Moon and Stars...
Made the trees and flowers too...
Tells the ocean how to flow...
So the tide comes back to you...

Created all the animals...
Both big and oh so small...
Takes care of our air and all of our needs...
Yes, He does it all...

Gives us the choice to follow Him...
To choose the right from wrong...
Lets us make those decisions...
And to Him...we truly belong...

Written by Margaret Bergeron
September 9, 2009

THE PRIZE...

It's not the prize I'm after...
Although it would be nice...
Writing words of honesty...
Giving great advice...

Telling what my heart feels...
Expressing thoughts and such...
Compared to that the grandest prize...
Doesn't matter very much...

However, those "Great words of praise"...
"Recognition of my time"...
"Being published" means the most...
Those rewards are, so sublime...

I would like my choice to be...
The unassuming prize...
Perhaps on the top seller list..
My poem book on the rise..!

Written by Margaret Bergeron
July 1999

YOU'VE WANDERED WITH ME...
TO THE LAST PAGE...

THE LAST PAGE...

I want to just say "Thank You All"...
For reading all the way...
Hope you know how much it means...
When you read the words I say...

Now you're on the last page...
You've... wandered... to the end...
Never fear...another book...
Is just around the bend...!

With Love,
Margaret Bergeron
2009

INDEX

With special thanks to my family...

Thank you to my Sister-in-Law, Kim McClinton
for painting my beautiful cover...

Thank you to our daughter Cari Ablondi for all of the great ideas...

Thank you to Les Ablondi for the help in editing...

Thank you to my dear friend, Judy Migliaccio, for the final editing.

To all of my friends and readers of the Mobile Home News...

A special thanks to my parents, John and Clarice
McClinton...for making me get this book published!

And a very special thank you to my husband, Billy, for listening to all
of the many hours of reading that it took to complete this book...

And, Thank You God, for giving me the Words, the
Faith and the Love to make this book...